AF379045

Published in the United States of America

Published by Authentic Creations a/ka/ Books and Swag

Cover Design: Libby Murphy

Library of Congress Cataloging-in-Publication-Data
Kaufmann, Kathryn Jane
ISBN:978-0-9651472-0-0

All scripture quotations are taken from THE LIVING BIBLE and Saint Joseph Edition of the NEW AMERICAN BIBLE. Grateful acknowledgement is made to Thomas Nelson Publishers for permission to reprint excerpts from previously published material: *It's Me O Lord* by William Bradford Huie, Copyright © 1979.

This is a nonfiction book. Written permission has been obtained. At the individuals' request, some of the names have been changed.

Manufactured in the United States of America

MARRIAGES MEANT TO BE

KATHRYN KAUFMANN

WHEN GOD CREATED MOTHERS, HE blessed me with the very best! I dedicate *Marriages Meant To Be* to my mother and best friend, Jane Lawson Kaufmann, whose love, support, and constant encouragement has held me together.

Mother, I hope and pray that all the good you have given will return to you one thousand fold!

Love,

Kathryn

In Loving Memory of:
My Father, Andrew Joseph Kaufmann

Your time on earth was short,
but your memories long and many,
I can't imagine you anywhere else,
but at God's Table of Plenty,
Though I've not physically seen your face since
November 1987
I can feel you peering down through the immaculate
windows of heaven,
By all your friends and family, you've certainly been
missed,
So look at me one moment,
I'm blowing up a kiss!

Let me never forget where I came from.
I will always be your girl!

And In Loving Memory of:
My Mother, Jane Kaufmann

Mom gained the privilege of celebrating her first
birthday in heaven on May 20th, 2016.
Forever missed, forever loved. Can't we to embrace
you when I reach the Above!

*From what God has shown, I have lived,
learned and grown!*

~ Kathryn Kaufmann

WITHOUT THE CONTRIBUTION OF THEIR unique marriage stories, this book would not exist. To each and every couple, whose stories make up the following pages, I thank you from the bottom of my heart. Your dedication and commitments to one another are hope and inspiration for all.

Table of Contents

FOREWARD

Originally, *Marriages Meant To Be* was published in 1997 before the Internet was heavily relied upon and social media existed. Without any major marketing, *Marriages Meant To Be* stood on its own merit. It was the topic of conversation on nineteen radio stations across the country and in Canada. It made a feature story in two newspapers and a mention in a magazine. I was invited on our local ABC and Fox affiliate stations to talk about the extraordinary stories written in *Marriages Meant To Be.*

I always believed if I'd had enough money to fund a marketing campaign, I could have given *Marriages Meant To Be* wings. But at that time, I was struggling financially just to buy food and gas. I couldn't even afford an afternoon matinee. So, sadly, my book promotions came to a halt.

Now…with the Internet in full bloom along with great social media sites to network, *Marriages Meant to Be* is being born again. The stories never grow old. They are as refreshing today as they were when I first collected them. And there are even a few more than before that I've added in the "Out Takes" section.

With the divorce rate on the rise, *Marriages Meant To Be* breathes new life into a world suffering from failed relationships and divorces that seem to make the daily headlines. It lends hope to singles searching to find "The One."

Amazingly enough, the manner in which I collected each chapter is a story within itself so I decided to include how I got the stories in the order I collected them. Not only were these couples' marriages meant to be, this entire book was meant to be.

Now…come join me on my journey and recapture the Spirit of how awesome God is and how He is the Finder and Matchmaker of true love.

LET THE JOURNEY BEGIN

IT WAS FATHER'S DAY WEEKEND. Ever since my dad passed away, I tried to be with my mother and brothers at that time so I flew from St. Petersburg, Florida to my hometown of Birmingham, Alabama for a short visit. That Sunday evening I had dinner with my mother and oldest brother, Andy, at one of Birmingham's finest restaurants.

Seated at the table behind us was a huge party. With all the Happy Father's Day balloons and cards, there was no doubt it was relatives gathered to celebrate the occasion.

We had almost finished eating dinner when an elderly lady from their group pulled her chair over to our table. My family and I had no idea what she was about to say or what suddenly prompted this unexpected visit; but I must admit, she had our undivided attention.

The woman moved close to my brother Andy, smiled at him, placed her hands around his upper left arm, and then began telling all of us what a wonderful life she'd had and how very much she enjoyed living. She shared several funny stories from her life's experiences, and at times, we were laughing hysterically. Though the lady appeared to be in her early eighties, her mind was sharp and young.

Minutes later, she pointed to her husband, who was standing across the room, and started into the wildest story I'd ever heard about how they met and married. When she finished, she commented on how good the Lord had been to them and what a blessed life they'd had. I could have cried. She was truly thankful for everything and gave God credit for it all.

The party she was with had closed out their dinner tab, and they were standing under the exit sign trying to get everyone together so they could leave. The woman never revealed her identity, but relatives began yelling, "Nancy, come on. Let's go, Nancy." It was at that moment I learned her name.

Nancy threw her hand in the air and hollered back in disgust, "All right. In a minute."

But her family was losing patience. On their final call, they threatened to carry her out of the restaurant. Having heard that, Nancy got up to leave; but before she did, she hugged our necks and stated what a pleasure it was meeting us and she hoped to see us again some day.

After returning to my home in St. Petersburg, Florida, I told all my friends about this neat lady, her amazing stories, and the unusual manner in which we met. They also agreed this encounter was quite extraordinary. I thought about Nancy often and wondered what she might be doing. If only I had gotten her telephone number or address, I could have kept in touch.

Two and a half years passed. Once again, I was traveling north to spend the holidays with my family. Instead of flying home, I chose to drive. With ten long hours ahead of me, I couldn't help but replay the horrific details of four months earlier, July 12th, 1994, which was still so fresh in my mind. After finishing a three mile jog that evening around the apartment complex where I resided, I was grabbed from behind, dragged into the woods, and thrown into a ditch by a complete stranger. Petrified, I shuddered, *Oh, no, he's going to rape and kill me.*

As the attacker tried desperately to restrain my hands around a tree with what he termed "buckles," I, in turn, fought for my life. The more I retaliated, the more violent he became. I was not only strangled, but slapped repeatedly. With hardly a breath left in me, I mercifully begged the attacker to leave. But that only resulted in a strike across my face with force strong enough to chip and crack my upper and lower front teeth.

As time stood still in the midst of what I believed to be a never ending struggle, pictures of yesteryears flashed through my mind like a video-tape in fast forward. Ponytails and pigtails seemed like last week, and kindergarten seemed only yesterday. Then my most sentimental childhood memory appeared in clear focus. A memory as simple as the day my father handed me a piece of Doublemint gum (telling me not to chew it until after school), then gave me a kiss good-bye as he let me out for first grade.

I felt I'd just arrived, and now my time on earth was over. I was saddened by all the things I would have to leave behind. *I wouldn't live to see my nieces and nephews grow up. What would it be like to not bid farewell to my friends? And, oh, no, what would my family think? How would they ever accept this or deal with this tragedy? How would my mother cope with losing her youngest child and only daughter?*

As the video of my life continued scanning through my mind, I thought about all the things I'd planned to do but had not yet accomplished, and how my whole twenty-nine years suddenly seemed like a fraction of a second. Then, all at once, the camera stopped rolling and the picture paused on my life at present.

I'd dreamed of being a writer. I had so many stories to tell of the miracles God had performed in my life. Even family and close friends had encouraged me on countless occasions to pursue my God-given talent. But, no, I let unimportant things block me from accelerating to the highest steps of success. And here I was lying helplessly in a ditch, my fate now resting in the hands of a killer.

Too tired to struggle any longer with my attacker, I was about to surrender to this inhumane and heinous crime that I never asked for or did anything in my life to deserve; but before I did, I gave a chance for freedom one more try, except this time I silently prayed: "*Dear God, I've not done what I'm supposed to do, and I'm not ready to die. If you'll grant me a second chance, I promise You, I'll go back and do everything You want me to do. I want to be a writer. Please send someone out here now to save me because I can't keep fighting.*"

After a prayer and a promise to God, the struggle that I'd deemed my final hour was over as fast as it had begun when, suddenly, a man from the apartment complex who had heard my screams, hollered through the woods, "Are you okay over there?" In an instant, my attacker fled, never to be apprehended. I was, and still am, forever grateful for being spared from rape and possibly death, and all the more determined to fulfill my obligation to the Lord.

Continuing up I-75 North on my way home for Thanksgiving, I racked my brain trying to decide what kind of book I would write. Because the attack was so traumatic, I couldn't read or watch anything that contained violence. I wanted my book to provide hope and inspiration for everyone and to help restore faith in humankind.

As I started nearing Gainesville, an idea exploded in my head. I became so excited the ten hour trip seemed like only two. That's when *Marriages Meant To Be* first came into focus. *There's my answer!* I thought. I'd heard unusual marriage stories my whole life, just like Nancy, the cute, elderly lady who'd pulled her chair over to our table at that restaurant on Father's Day and began telling me and my family how she met her husband. Now all I had to do was find these people and collect their stories.

And as I pray for God's hand in everything, I also asked Him to help me make this project possible. Nothing is ever as we expect it. I had my own plan in mind, but the Lord had another.

After the Thanksgiving holiday was over, I returned to Florida, and it appeared my court reporting career was about to crumble, at least in the Tampa/St. Petersburg area. There was no need to be alarmed because we'd just celebrated Thanksgiving, and Christmas was rapidly approaching. Everyone was festive and in no mood to work. Before panicking, I figured I'd give this deposition defunct until the first of the year to improve.

Even then, work was so scarce, I feared I might have to relocate. And that old gut-wrenching feeling was churning inside me saying, *If you don't give in and get back to Birmingham, life could become painstakingly miserable.* Aside from being attacked, I loved Florida and dreaded the thought of leaving. But if I had to relocate for employment purposes, I wanted to move to Alabama. That was home. Besides, I was trying to readjust and deal with the emotional turmoil I'd suffered from the incident and had no desire to start over again in a city where I had no family or childhood friends.

I've always known God will guide you and give signs when it's time for a change. And believe me, I was getting some pretty powerful indications a move was on the horizon. For instance, the court reporting firm where I was employed had a minimal amount of work, so I contacted several other agencies. Every place I called had recently hired a new reporter or didn't have enough work to keep their regular employees busy.

On one of my attempts to seek local employment, the woman I spoke with about a potential job got such a tickle in her throat while trying to interview me over the phone, she hacked until she almost threw up. I waited a few minutes to see if she could catch her breath long enough to complete the conversation, but no such luck. The woman mumbled something in a raspy, choking voice, then hung up. I contemplated dialing 911, but I was certain she would be fine. As far as I was concerned, her choking episode was just another telltale sign that I needed to extricate myself from the area.

Then came the Grand Finale. Whenever I was fortunate enough to have a scheduled deposition, the job would cancel once I got there, then I couldn't charge the client. One afternoon I waited forty-five minutes. Finally the attorney entered the conference room and informed me the deposition had canceled earlier in the day. He apologized for failing to notify our offices and for me having to make the trip. These canceled depositions were beginning to feel like bomb drops. I could not afford to keep this up. One more and I would become stiff competition for the *Will Work for Food* sign guys.

That afternoon, I drove home, dragged into my apartment and fell onto my bed. I had reached my wit's end. I reflected back to the conversation I had days earlier with a gentleman at a court reporting firm in Birmingham, who I contacted regarding possible employment. At that time he stated they were not too busy, work had slowed down during the Christmas holidays and had not yet picked up. The man was well aware of my financial concerns, and he promised to contact me as soon as business resumed to normal.

I lay on my bed, staring up into the ceiling fan. Silently, I prayed: *"Okay, God, if it's in Your will for me to move home…You know I don't want to leave Florida…but if that's what You really want me to do, then let that man from Birmingham call and tell me he's got enough work to keep me busy, and I will go."*

In less than ten minutes, the telephone rang. Half asleep and worried sick about what to do, I nearly jumped out of my skin. I remember thinking, *What if that's the guy from Birmingham,* and lo and behold, it was. I could hardly believe my ears. Almost breathless, I exclaimed to him, "I just prayed about whether or not to move."

I'll never forget his response: "That's why I'm calling you. I just checked with my office and they don't have enough reporters to cover the depositions. I've got enough work to keep you busy if you want to come home."

He wasn't even in Birmingham when he contacted me. He was on an assignment in Mobile. My prayer was answered so instantly and powerfully, I felt I better take heed and move my rear end north...and soon.

I knew all along it was the Lord's will for me to move home, but I was going to fight Him until the bitter end. Well, guess Who won? I hired a group of men to load my belongings into the back of a moving van and drive it all the way to Alabama.

So here I was, another city, different state and a new place of employment. One thing I liked most about the job was I had my own office in a high-rise building downtown. No longer would I have to wrestle with the boredom of working out of my home like many court reporters do. Once I caught up with transcribing testimony, I could work on my book. I had a handful of stories to begin the project, but I needed many more.

Thoughts of Nancy, the spunky older woman from years past, weighed heavily on my mind. More than anything, I wished to locate her and seek permission to publish their marriage story, but I didn't know her last name or anyone who knew her. I was clueless where to even begin looking. As I tossed ideas around in my mind, I recalled a comment my brother Andy made the evening we met Nancy. He stated that her husband was "big into Alabama football." Well, in the South, that statement is considered generic. Many Alabamians are "big into Alabama football." As far as I was concerned, that expression was of little importance and was not going to help me at all.

The search began with my mother. I telephoned her and asked if she remembered the evening we met Nancy, and if, by chance, she recalled the couple's last name. I reminded her of the comment my brother made. I was surprised when she announced their name without hesitation. I thanked her repeatedly, then opened the phone book and found the listing.

I started to dial the number. Suddenly, I felt like a complete idiot. *How would I explain this? Would Nancy remember me from a brief encounter? Would she still be alive? What if something happened to her?* I then reassured myself these were risks I had to take if I wanted to achieve my goal.

On the second ring, a gentleman answered. "May I speak to Nancy?" I asked.

There was a pause. "Nancy?"

"Yes, sir," I replied.

Solemnly, he responded, "Honey, Nancy died a year ago. This is Fred."

With that news, you could have buried me. All I could say was, "I'm sorry," and I hung up.

Afterwards, I had an overwhelming compulsion to write Fred and explain the reason I called. Before five o'clock that afternoon, I had mailed him a letter. I described the night I met Nancy and recited their marriage story as she related it to me. Then I gave a brief description about my book and asked permission to print the story.

When I came in from work the next day, there was a message on my answering machine. Fred had received my letter and sounded ecstatic over the idea of having his and Nancy's story published. We made arrangements to meet the following Monday at his sporting goods store in the local mall. I wanted to introduce myself and discuss the story, as I heard it, making sure it would be accurate.

When I arrived that morning, Fred greeted me with a kiss on the cheek. Then he escorted me into his office and pulled two chairs side by side for our interview.

I looked around. Trophies and awards from years past to present filled his office. Pictures of him with prominent people such as the legendary Coach Paul "Bear" Bryant covered the walls. I had no idea this man was a such a celebrity.

After I browsed over his honors and awards, we sat down and Fred began telling the story of how he met Nancy. Once in a while, a tear would roll down his face. When he expressed how much he missed her, a golf-ball size lump developed in my throat. It was all I could do to hold back my own tears. But somehow, we managed to make it through.

When the interview was over and I was about to leave, Fred turned to me and said, "You're my buddy now. Don't let it end here. You call me. I consider you my friend." I felt extremely honored.

When I met Nancy, the thought of writing *Marriages Meant To Be* had not yet developed, but I believe there is a reason for everything. I always wondered what compelled that woman to pull her chair over to our table that Father's Day evening and begin talking to total strangers. Now I know. Nancy, along with her story, confirms what I've always known to be true: We are led to certain places at certain times for certain reasons. When the seed was planted in my mind to write this book, this incredible story is what laid the foundation and helped turn my idea into reality.

To Nancy and Fred Sington, this special tribute I dedicate. Though you have passed before us, your spirits still remain. The story you loved to tell is now being written for all the world to see. Both of you touched my life in ways you'll never know, and I thank you!

THE WHEEL OF FORTUNE

I T WAS JUNE OF 1932. Nancy Napier had recently graduated from the University of Georgia. And like any college graduate who doesn't have a job waiting for them, Nancy was curious as to where life's road would lead her.

She had always been fascinated with fortune tellers. Though she had never before visited one, she knew many friends who had. Nancy was most intrigued with a woman well known throughout Georgia for her accurate predictions. The psychic was said to be so phenomenal, the people of Atlanta swore by her augury. The fortune teller worked at a wallpaper company. In her spare time, she read Tarot cards. Nancy had heard of the woman ever since she was a small child. As a young adult, she was ready to pay her a visit.

Nancy had a close male friend named Johnnie Harper. Their relationship was strictly platonic. Johnnie was well aware of Nancy's infatuation with psychics, and with her desire to call that particular woman, so he promised to accompany Nancy to see the fortune teller should she decide to make an appointment. That was all the encouragement Nancy Napier needed.

One summer evening in June of 1932, the two of them struck out to visit the woman. Being Nancy's first time to see a fortune teller, she was a bit nervous. But the lady's warm smile and pleasant greeting put her at ease. The woman invited Johnnie and Nancy into her home and escorted them into a place she called the reading room. Once they sat down, the fortune teller began shuffling the cards. She, in turn, asked Nancy to cut the deck.

The soothsayer began laying the cards in a pattern that was foreign to Nancy and Johnnie. Then she began to read them from the layout. "My, oh, my," said the woman. "You've got quite a surprise coming to you," she added.

Nancy gripped the edge of her seat.

The woman continued. "You're going to meet a man soon. He's going to be very tall with dark hair, and extremely handsome. He's a very big guy, and he's heavily involved in athletics. You will begin to date." The psychic further exclaimed, "Oh, and another surprise. You'll be married before Christmas of this year."

Nancy was shocked, and at the same time, disappointed. The woman's prediction did not come remotely close to what Nancy expected to hear. First of all, she wasn't looking to get married. Secondly, she had no interest in sports, nor was she the least bit athletically inclined. Nancy was disgusted and thought, *What in the world will I have in common with this man?*

Johnnie spoke up, "She's really not interested in that kind of deal. Could you run the cards again?"

"Okay. But I can only tell you what the cards reveal," said the fortune teller.

At Johnnie's request, the woman ran the Tarot cards a second time, repeating the same procedure of shuffling, having Nancy cut the deck, then placing the cards down in a layout. Amazingly, the second reading was identical to the first. The exact same cards appeared in the subsequent layout. The psychic was adamant when explaining, "I'm sorry, this is what the cards reveal. Now that's as much as I can tell you. You're going to meet this man and be married before Christmas."

As far as Nancy was concerned, this entire prediction was merely hogwash. She could not imagine how any of this could be possible. Johnnie and Nancy thanked the fortune teller for her time, then left. On the drive home,

Nancy could not keep quiet and constantly complained that their visit to the psychic was nothing but a wasted trip. She even blurted, "I don't know how she managed to conjure up such a bowl of crap."

Later in the week, Nancy's girlfriend, Caroline, wanted to set her up on a blind date. Caroline's steady boyfriend, Bob, had a good buddy named Fred who lived nearby. The two boys had grown up together. Bob also knew Nancy Napier was not involved with any one particular beau so he insisted on introducing her to Fred. Besides, he and Caroline thought it would be fun to double date. When Bob approached Fred with the idea, he was certainly amenable. And Nancy, of course, had no qualms with the idea.

Late Thursday afternoon, Bob gave Fred directions to Nancy's house; and that Friday evening, he drove to Atlanta's Five Points to pick her up. She lived in a beautiful home with a huge front porch. As Fred got out of the car and started up the sidewalk, he could see a girl standing on the front steps. It was Nancy. She began waving her arms above her head and hollering, "Don't come up here. If you do, you'll have to marry me before Christmas."

Needless to say, Fred was flabbergasted. He stopped in his tracks, and with the most startled look on his face, he responded, "Sugar, I didn't come here to marry you. I just came to take you to the picture show. That's all."

Why Fred had never laid eyes on this girl before tonight, and thoughts of marrying her certainly never entered his mind. Of course Fred was unaware of Nancy's trip to the soothsayer. And she, remembering the guru's words, was only being facetious with her theatrics and comment. But just as the psychic predicted, Fred *was* big and tall, and his hair *was* dark. And, yes, he was also extremely handsome.

He made his way to the front porch. And soon after

the two became acquainted, they were en route to the Fox Theater to meet Bob and Caroline.

It's assumed Nancy enjoyed Fred's company that evening because she pled guilty to the oldest trick in the book. She intentionally left her purse in his car as an excuse to see him again.

The next day Fred returned to Nancy's home with the purse. There he was introduced to Nancy's mother who happened to be a baseball fanatic. What a coincidence! He was originally from Alabama, but Fred's sole purpose in Atlanta was to play baseball. So with Fred being a member of the Atlanta Crackers baseball team and Ms. Napier a big fan, they hit it off from the start. Another one of the fortune teller's predictions had just proven true. The statement, "He'll be heavily involved in athletics," was echoing through Nancy's mind.

But there was much more to Fred's athletic abilities than Nancy was aware. Fred Sington already had quite a list of accomplishments. Baseball wasn't the only sport Fred was involved in. He attended the University of Alabama from 1927-1931, where he was a two-sport star athlete lettering in baseball and football. Fred's football record was so outstanding, Knute Rockne, the legendary Notre Dame coach, titled Fred "the greatest lineman in America."

During his senior year of college in 1931, before air transportation, the Alabama Crimson Tide rode the train to Pasadena, California to play in the Rose Bowl. Will Rogers emceed the opening ceremonies where Alabama beat Washington State 24-0, and, of course, Fred was the star player. Later Nancy learned Fred's nickname was *Football Freddy*, derived from Rudy Valle's 1930 hit song, *Football, Freddy, rugged and tan. Football, Freddy, All American Man.*

Fred's athletic abilities were so outstanding, he received a two page telegram from Hollywood while still in college. They offered to pay him $800 a week to star in a movie titled *The All-American*. Fred informed the coach and teammates that he would soon be leaving for California. He said he thought he might better let the school president know too; but when he shared the good news with him, the president handed out some free advice. "You've done so well in school, son. If you go to Hollywood, there's always the possibility they'll just ruin your life. You're involved with student government. You made Phi Beta Kappa and are a top academic honorary. Hollywood could be a mistake. If you finish your education, no one can ever take that away from you."

After giving careful thought to the school president's suggestion, Fred decided against going to the entertainment capital of the world. He was so ecstatic over being offered a major role in a Hollywood film, he didn't stop to evaluate the consequences. Looking back, Fred stated he was glad he didn't go to California; he might have missed meeting Nancy.

Initially, Nancy never believed a word the psychic said. But, ironically, a third prediction came true. They began dating steady. Through the months of June, July and August, they were together every minute that Fred wasn't playing baseball. Then fall rolled around and Fred left Atlanta and headed to North Carolina where he would be coaching football at Duke University. Nancy remained in Georgia, but they corresponded through letters.

In October, Fred returned to Atlanta to visit Nancy. He explained that he would be traveling around the country playing baseball in the summers and coaching football during the fall and winters. He did not wish to live apart any longer and the problem was solved instantly when Fred and Nancy decided to get married.

By now, Nancy was convinced the fortune teller had been pretty accurate, especially when they tied the knot before Christmas of that same year — December 4th, 1932 to be exact.

After they married, Fred took Nancy on a real tour of life within the world of sports. First, the Atlanta Crackers, a Southern league, sold Fred to the Washington Senators, an American league. Then Washington sold him to the Brooklyn Dodgers. Finally, a National league! Then in 1941, Fred joined the Navy. They sent him to Oklahoma where he was named head football coach of the Oklahoma Zoomers. When his coaching career ended at Oklahoma, he left for San Diego to coach baseball.

Before meeting Fred, Nancy was oblivious to sports, but soon, outside recreation became her life. In baseball, Fred said she learned to track score better than the scorekeepers. Fred also spoke of some of the foolishness Nancy had to put up with. Once when he struck out, Nancy overheard some lady sitting in the box seat say, "Well, he was out all night drinking. No wonder he couldn't hit."

Nancy became furious and quickly jumped to Fred's defense. "Oh, just shut up and mind your own business," Nancy told her. She didn't put up with much nonsense, especially a derogatory comment directed towards her husband.

After Fred's many years of traveling and coaching football and playing professional baseball, he and Nancy decided it was time to move back South. They returned to Fred's home in Birmingham, Alabama where he opened Fred Sington's Sporting Goods store. Fred and Nancy had three sons who followed in their father's footsteps, all excellent athletes.

Words cannot define the wonderful life Fred and Nancy Sington shared together. As for Nancy, she never believed a word the soothsayer said when she read the Tarot cards for her back in June of 1932; but, coincidentally, about the only thing the woman didn't foretell

while predicting Nancy's *Wheel of Fortune* is that she and
the big, tall, dark and handsome athlete would be married 62 years—1932-1994!

HOW I COLLECTED:
A TRIP TO TREASURE

HERE IT WAS THE MIDDLE of February. I was freezing to death. Who in their right mind would leave warm and sunny St. Pete, Florida to relocate north in the throes of winter? Well, I had an option. I could have stayed in Florida, kept warm and gone broke or I could sacrifice the warm weather to be able to pay the bills. It just made so much more sense to struggle through the winter and maintain financial stability.

I started re-evaluating that situation as I stared out my office window. The fog was so thick and heavy, I could barely see the surrounding office buildings. Misting rain only added more gray to the already doom and gloom picture. So I decided to take a mid-morning break.

After a sixteen ounce bottle of soda, my first destination was the bathroom. As I entered the restroom, so did a co-worker named Judy. She asked me what I had been so hard at work on. I guess Judy could see when passing my office, I wasn't transcribing depositions. As I began explaining *Marriages Meant To Be,* a woman in one of the stalls, who could not help overhearing our conversation, spoke up, "Hey, I've got a story for you."

Talk about unusual. While we're using the facilities, this woman, who I'd yet to see, began telling me a unique marriage story. As she continued, the story got even better, especially when she said, "See…I'm not even from Birmingham. I just moved here from Tampa, Florida."

For a moment, I thought I'd been struck by a bolt of lightning. To be so homesick for Florida, and to be making a friend from my old stomping grounds at the same time, was electrifying. At last, while at the lavatory, I came face to face with this fun and crazy girl who introduced herself as Julie Jewett. Before we parted, I asked permission to print the story. Julie said she would be honored.

Meeting Julie was a package deal. Not only did I make a friend from Florida, I collected another chapter for my book. Julie's marriage story proves that timing is everything, much like our encounter in the ladies room that day.

A TRIP TO TREASURE

JULIE JEWETT WAS JUST SEVEN years old when her parents divorced. When she turned twelve, rumors ran rampant in the town of Wheeling, West Virginia that employee layoffs were a possibility at the hospital where Julie's mother was a nurse.

Being a single mom and having to support three daughters, Ms. Jewett could take no chances. She quickly began searching for a job elsewhere. After countless interviews, she accepted a position in Tampa, Florida. The only disadvantage was the hundreds of miles distance between the girls and their father.

But every summer, Julie and her sisters Jamie and Jodie returned to Wheeling to visit their dad. While there, they also got together with childhood friends. But this particular summer turned out a little different than those in the past. On June 23rd, 1993, Julie, Jamie and Missy, a lifelong friend of theirs, visited a local college tavern they had never set foot in before.

They had just walked inside the place when Jamie Jewett noticed a bald-headed man across the bar. Though she was not interested in the guy, she knew her sister Julie would be. Indeed, an enigma because what oftentimes is a major turn-off to most women was a definite thumbs-up for Julie. Even Julie could never explain the reason behind such magnetism. Her only theory was a balding appearance gave men a more distinguished and sophisticated look.

Whatever the case, Jamie nudged Julie on the shoulder and kiddingly said, "Look! There's a bald-headed man for you."

Jamie was surprised when the guy got out of his chair and approached them. She didn't have a clue this man knew their good friend Missy. His name was Ed Gornik. And he basically invited himself into the conversation by saying, "Hey, Missy! I've never seen you in here before."

But Ed didn't spend much time talking to Missy and Jamie. It was obvious he took an immediate interest in Julie. With her tall, slender figure, shiny brown hair and sparkling brown eyes, she could have her pick. Ed asked Julie questions like, "What are you doing in West Virginia? Most people go to Tampa for vacation."

When she told him she was born and raised in Wheeling and was visiting relatives, Ed's jaw dropped. He, too, was born and raised in Wheeling. The more they talked, the more coincidences surfaced. At the age of twelve – the same age Julie was when she left West Virginia – Ed left the state when his father accepted a job in Birmingham, Alabama. After high school graduation, he returned to West Virginia, lived with his grandmother and attended Wheeling Jesuit College where he was going into his senior year.

Next they uncovered the fact that both attended Wheeling Park Recreation Day Camp at the same time but had no recollection of each other. The only thing they could remember about camp was the simple fact that you couldn't bring your own milk; you had to buy it there so it wouldn't spoil in the heat. Even sillier, you could bring your own lunch and store it in their refrigerator; you didn't have to purchase lunch at the day camp.

They stood no chance of being classmates during the regular school year because Ed attended St. Vincent's Catholic and Julie was enrolled at the public school. Similarities between the two seemed endless.

Ed and Julie became so engrossed in conversation, they lost track of time. It was two o'clock in the morning when they closed the tavern, but they didn't part ways without exchanging telephone numbers and addresses.

When the girls arrived home, they found their father waiting up, curious as to why they strolled in at such a late hour. Seeing the girls were fine, they all sat down. Julie told her father about the magic evening. "Dad, you would just never believe the guy I met tonight. He moved away from Wheeling the same year I did, but he came back to go to school."

At first, Mr. Jewett was as perplexed as any father would be. But as Julie revealed more information about Ed, her father discovered something unusual. He knew many of Ed's relatives including the grandmother Ed was currently residing with. Furthermore, he remembered Ed's grandfather who was the mailman for many years. As it turned out, Julie's father was childhood friends with Ed's Uncle David, too. And that wasn't all. Mr. Jewett realized he taught Ed's uncle how to swim at the old water hole in the neighborhood where they grew up.

Then another coincidence surfaced in this bizarre turn of events. Before Julie's family moved to Florida and Ed's family relocated to Alabama, their parents were friends. They socialized on occasion and belonged to the same bowling league. Learning all of this put Julie's father at ease. Mr. Jewett no longer had to worry about his daughter spending time with a total stranger. Gosh, he felt like he'd known Ed all his life. So did Julie!

The two love birds didn't miss a day of seeing each other during Julie's visit to Wheeling. But the dreaded return to Tampa was rapidly approaching and it would be August before Julie could see Ed again. To make the two months separation less painful, Ed surprised Julie by traveling to Florida for a visit. They toured the state together. Busch Gardens, Adventure Island and Cypress Gardens were only a few of their stops. But their most special moments together were spent at the beach.

One evening, while watching a beautiful sunset over the Gulf of Mexico, and wrapped in a warm embrace, Ed whispered "Will you marry me" in Julie's ear. The answer was obvious.

Though Ed was leaving the next evening, he wasn't too concerned about when Julie would visit her father again because he knew she'd soon become his wife. On August 3rd, 1996 in Wheeling, West Virginia – where both were born, raised, removed and reunited – Ed and Julie Gornik were married!

INTRODUCTION TO:
A TWIST OF FATE

THOUGH I HATED SAYING GOOD-BYE to my friends in Florida, moving to Alabama gave me a chance to say hello to many old, but familiar faces. One of them being Gaye Henderson Mobley. Our friendship began in first grade and extends way beyond cap and gown.

We found humor in everything we did. We discussed our hopes and dreams. We talked about what kind of husbands we wanted and imagined how we might come to meet them some day. We were both big believers in fate and destiny. It was on a flight home from a weekend visit to New York City when Gaye told me how her parents met and married. I never dreamed that many moons ago that I would one day write their love story in a book.

Now back in Alabama, I had the perfect opportunity to collect it so I called Gaye's mom and scheduled an interview. When it came to having a mate, for Rod and Nancy Henderson it was a *"Twist of Fate!"*

A TWIST OF FATE

IN 1956, WHEN MOST SEVENTEEN year old girls were necking with their special beau at the drive-in movie, Nancy Sibley sweet-talked her dates into teaching her how to operate their standard shift vehicle. So when her older sister, Joyce, bought a '55 Chevy, but couldn't drive it, Nancy's experience with four on the floor came in quite handy. While Joyce drove through the neighborhood, Nancy sat on the passenger's side and instructed her on how to switch gears. After a few lessons, Joyce felt confident enough to travel on a major thoroughfare.

With the afternoon drawing towards an end, and the sun setting on the west side of Atlanta, Nancy, Joyce, and two of their friends were en route for the big city. They wound up at the world's largest drive-in restaurant, the Varsity. Just down the street from Georgia Tech University, the Varsity attracted many teens and college students.

As soon as Joyce pulled in and parked, the girls ordered their favorite delicacies—*walk a dog sideways* with *bags of rags* on the side. Translated, that meant a hot dog with onions and a bag of potato chips.

While the girls waited for their order, crowds gathered around to compliment and admire Joyce Sibley's new set of wheels, but the most interested onlookers happened to be a group of guys. Of course, they weren't just inspecting the outside of the vehicle. Nothing would do until they hopped in the back seat and examined the four beautiful girls inside.

While the other guys gibbered with Joyce and her

two friends, their buddy, the tall, thin, brown-haired boy obviously had eyes for Nancy. He flirted with her for an hour but never once gave his name, nor did she. Unfortunately, the party had to end when the girls announced they needed to get home. Bless Joyce's heart, with Nancy as her driver's education teacher, she successfully drove them to the Varsity. But still inexperienced, she had second thoughts about backing down the steep hill. The last thing she needed to do was accidentally roll into a couple of vehicles and wreck her '55 Chevy.

The guy who'd been so fixated on Nancy overheard Joyce say she was afraid to pull out. He politely turned to her and said, "Move over and I'll back it out for you."

The girls didn't know his name, but they certainly accepted his offer. When the boy put the car in reverse and began backing out, his friends applauded and cheered, "I hear you, *Captain Mellowfruit*. Way to go, buddy!"

Certainly *Captain Mellowfruit* was not the fellow's name. These witty boys were imitating the product carrier for Mellowfruit gum. The popular television commercial in the late Fifties pictured a lady tied to railroad tracks, a train moving rapidly in her direction. Foreseeing the danger, *Captain Mellowfruit* placed a stick of the gum in his mouth, which provided him an enormous amount of strength. Just before the train could strike the lady, *Captain Mellowfruit*, now built of iron muscle, untied the woman and heroically rescued her from the tracks.

Though this young man didn't rescue Nancy and Joyce from railroad tracks, he did prevent them from possibly slamming into a half dozen other vehicles. Since they still didn't know his real name, they identified him as *Captain Mellowfruit*. Once he'd finished a job well done, the girls thanked him, then waved good-bye. Nancy Sibley thought nothing of ever seeing him again.

About six months later, she got a telephone call from

Mary Nell Intra, a dear friend of hers who ran a boardinghouse in Douglasville, Georgia. Mary Nell had no children, so she posed as a mother figure for everyone else's. "Nancy, I've got someone I want you to meet."

Naturally, Nancy wanted to know more. "Well, Mary Nell, what's his name and what does he look like?" she asked.

"Well, his name is Rod Henderson. He's my sweet little ol' boy, Nancy, and you've just gotta meet him! I'll tell you what I'm gonna do. I'll bring him over to your house."

Nancy had known Mary Nell for many years and completely trusted her judgment. In her opinion, if Mary Nell claimed Rod as her "sweet little ol' boy," that meant he was the angel in her class, and Mary Nell had taken him under her wing. Nancy told her if she wanted to bring Rod over, that would be fine. Douglasville was about twenty-five miles from Atlanta, so they made arrangements for that Friday.

As always, Mary Nell was prompt. About 7:00 that evening, the doorbell rang and Nancy went to answer it. There stood Mary Nell and her "sweet little ol' boy," Rod. Nancy invited them inside; and before Mary Nell could introduce them, Rod exclaimed, "I know you! I backed your sister's car off the hill at the Varsity a few months ago. Remember?"

Up until now, Nancy had forgotten about the girls' joy ride to Atlanta. "Wait a minute! Yes, I do remember. You're *Captain Mellowfruit!*" she shouted.

Mary Nell stood speechless. *What in the world was going on here,* she wondered. So she would understand, Rod and Nancy took a few moments and explained their previous encounter. Of course, Mary Nell, the matchmaker, was shocked to discover the couple she eagerly wished to introduce had crossed paths once before.

And how would Nancy have ever guessed that Mary

Nell's "sweet little ol' boy" was actually the fellow who backed her sister's car out at the Varsity?

Rod recalled that evening quite well. After rescuing the girls from potential disaster and waving good-bye as they drove off, he remembered Nancy in a special way: *hair of gold, eyes of blue, there's no other girl as pretty as you.* Though he would have liked to, Rod never actually expected to see blue eyes again, so the outcome of this introduction certainly caught him by surprise.

Of course, Mary Nell didn't plan on being a third wheel. Because Rod worked two jobs to put himself through school, he had sacrificed many luxuries, including a vehicle. Being the sweetheart that she was, Mary Nell arranged to visit Nancy's parents, Mr. and Mrs. Sibley, and loaned Rod her car for the evening.

Undoubtedly, Mary Nell Intra was in the wrong business. Instead of running a boardinghouse and selling movie tickets on weekends, she should have managed a dating service. A year later, after announcing their engagement, Rod and Nancy rushed to the theater and told the matchmaker their good news. Mary Nell jumped from her chair and ran out of the ticket booth to hug and congratulate them. No way in this world would she miss the big event.

On June 23rd, 1957, Rod and Nancy became one before God, their family and friends.

Brought together by a *Twist of Fate*, having lived their lives according to Biblical principles, and raising four children in a fine Christian home, Rod and Nancy Henderson's forty plus years of marriage remained as smooth and solid as the ice they skated their first date on.

Giving credit where credit is due, the Hendersons apply their success to Psalms 128:1-4: "Blessings on all who reverence and trust the Lord—on all who obey him! Their reward shall be prosperity and happiness. Your wife shall be contented in your home. And look at all those children. There they sit around the dinner table as vigorous and healthy as young olive trees. That is God's reward to those who reverence and trust Him."

A PATH WITH NO WARNING SIGNS

While traveling down the path of life you'll make some crazy turns, some will be wrong, some right; but nevertheless, you'll learn,
They'll be many an obstacle in your path causing you to swerve,
Just grab the wheel and hold on tight when rounding those blind curves,
Once you're on the straight and narrow, don't think you've escaped all strife,
Because right about that moment,
Look up! Look out! There's life!
—Kathryn Kaufmann

TO SUM UP HOW CRAZY and chaotic my life had once again become, I composed *A Path With No Warning Signs.* By now it was April, 1995. Once I'd started thawing out from the frosty winter, thanks to the pollen, I began sneezing my way through spring.

Just when I thought I had dodged the jagged edges and bypassed rough pavement with the hope of sailing along smoothly, it appeared history was beginning to repeat itself because my job was not only turning into a nightmare, but the faces of George Washington, Abraham Lincoln and Benjamin Franklin were rapidly vanishing from my checking account.

My only theory to this unexplainable mess: God had a purpose for me in Alabama—though I hadn't quite figured His reason—so He created a job, for the time being, just to get me there. Since writing was my only escape to sanity in the midst of all the strife, I began collecting the next few chapters, which were stories I'd heard through the years from friends and relatives.

FAIRY TALE FANTASIES

ORTY-THREE YEAR OLD NANCY OLSEN had given up on ever finding a life-long companion. She was highly successful in her court reporting career. Unfortunately, her luck with men was just the opposite. On and off, she'd been involved in serious relationships, but none ever seemed strong or healthy enough to bind the bonds of marriage.

Like most bachelorettes, she'd dreamed her knight in shining armor would one day rescue her from a desolate singles' world. But after adopting the title *losers* to describe the type men she dated, her chances of finding a desirable partner were slim to none. All her adult life, Nancy became involved with guys that had drinking problems, which later led to financial problems. She'd never forget the time she loaned a boyfriend a thousand dollars. She never saw the money nor the man again.

The day came when Nancy wised up and realized, *Hey, I could be single the rest of my life, and I accept that fact, so I'd better learn to enjoy things on my own and stop waiting for a husband. From now on, I'm not dating any man that is not emotionally and financially stable.* So adamant about this, Nancy even confided to her close friend Amy that as far as her personal life, she was turning over a new leaf.

To beat the blues and avoid the lulls of loneliness, Nancy enrolled in sailing and golf classes at a local junior college, the two things she always wanted to learn, but never took the time to do, mainly because she was too chicken to go alone. These activities not only occupied her mind, they filled her social calendar. On weekends, if Nancy wasn't sailing, you could bet she was on the golf course with friends.

However, the turning point came one Saturday when Nancy's golfing match was canceled due to bad weather. To catch up on work and meet important deadlines, she stayed home and proofread depositions, that is until an interesting telephone call interrupted her concentration. It was a local dating service soliciting new clients.

Normally Nancy wouldn't give telephone solicitors the time of day; however, the sales pitch was exceptionally convincing, and an offer she couldn't refuse. For just half price, Nancy could obtain a lifetime membership. The sales representative persuaded her further by giving background information on some of the eligible bachelors—doctors, lawyers, and engineers—with salaries that tripled hers.

It all sounded good, but before Nancy Olsen would get suckered into anything, she was going to call her good friend Amy Carlisle, who, at one time, was a member of the same dating service. That fact alone raised Nancy's suspicion. Perhaps her good friend had something to do with this call. After all, Amy Carlisle was well aware of Nancy's past dating predicaments, so it made perfect sense she was only trying to help by supplying them Nancy's name and number.

No sooner did Nancy hang up from speaking with the sales rep than she telephoned Amy Carlisle. "Do you remember that dating service you used to belong to?"

"Yeah. Why?" Amy asked.

"You didn't give them my name, did you?"

Amy sounded appalled. "Are you kidding? I would never give out that type of information without consulting you first."

Nancy explained how the call came from out of the blue and was half kidding when she told Amy, "Maybe it's fate because if it hadn't been raining today, I would have played golf and missed the call."

Both girls were awe-struck over such an odd coincidence. And what an opportune time for a dating service to solicit new clients, not long after Nancy had sworn off the entire male population.

Because of Amy's familiarity with this particular organization, Nancy sought her opinion on whether to become a member. There's no doubt Amy had the right advice, "Nancy, you have nothing to lose and everything to gain. Even if you don't find a husband, you'll at least meet new people, not to mention, it will remove you from a rut and help get you back into circulation."

Within a week, Nancy signed up. Her first introduction was to a guy named John, who was recently divorced and not too eager to settle down. Ironically, her second introduction was also named John, but this *John* had a different story. He had been divorced nineteen years and was looking for a steady companion.

Nancy had every reason to be overwhelmingly impressed with John Jenkins after their first date. He seemed to have all the qualities she desired, two important ones being emotional and financial stability. For the last seventeen years, John had owned and operated a medical consulting firm. Finally, it appeared there could be light at the end of Nancy's dark and lonely tunnel. Best of all, Nancy's good humor and intellect sparked John's interest and he continued asking her out. It didn't take long for them to discover they had much in common. For instance, their ideas and views about life, politics, social issues and religion were one in the same. They shared the same taste in music and art. Even when it came to picking a movie, there was never any argument.

And after two years of steady dating, this romance seemed too good to be true. All Nancy could think about were past failed relationships, and she worried, sooner or later, history would repeat itself. Fortunately, Amy provided her with the support and encouragement she needed, always there to remind her, *Nancy, this time is going to be different.* And it was.

On July 4th, 1993, while fireworks displayed all over America, so did they in the Virgin Islands where John and Nancy exchanged marriage vows at a small, quaint church overlooking the ocean.

Needless to say, they neither one had to depend on the local dating service again, and both agreed that was one of the best investments they'd ever made.

However, there was a secret to Nancy's success that she never revealed until a few years after her wedding. Long before Nancy met John, she had started attending self-help seminars and learned if you wrote on paper, in specific detail, everything you wanted and hoped for, visualized it coming true for you, eventually it would. Many times Nancy seriously considered trying this technique, but had little faith it would work for her.

So approximately one year before the dating service solicited Nancy as a client, she finally put this advice to good use and made a list of everything she desired in a man. Periodically, she would get together with another friend who had done the same. They would light a white candle and meditate, envisioning their dreams as reality.

One of Nancy's fantasies was to meet a man who would take her to faraway places. Slowly, but surely, Nancy's travel wishes came to fruition. While honeymooning in the British Virgin Isles, she and John sipped Pina Colodas on every island. On their first year anniversary, they toured British Columbia.

Christmas 1994 was Nancy's best ever! She and John vacationed at Villa Caletas, a hotel high atop the mountains of Costa Rica. From their room, the view was magnificent. Not only were they overlooking the bright, blue Pacific

Ocean, they could see 360 degrees around the country. During Thanksgiving 1995, Nancy was grateful for plenty. John escorted her on their first trip to the green rolling hills of Ireland.

And last, but certainly not least, another of Nancy's wishes came true. Before marrying John, Nancy lived in a one bedroom condo. She longed to live in a large waterfront home. It just so happened that John owned a four bedroom house that overlooked Tampa Bay. The swimming pool, pier, deck boat, and jacuzzi were an added bonus.

After getting married, Nancy became so busy with her new life and trips abroad, she'd forgotten about the wish list she'd made the year prior to meeting John. But an interesting thing happened when she was spring cleaning in April of 1995. While sorting through old items, carefully separating the trash from her treasures, Nancy stumbled upon a sheet of paper that had been neatly folded and tucked away in a dresser drawer. Curious, she pulled it out. Much to her surprise, it was the wish list. But even more surprising was the fact that everything Nancy asked for, right down to the specifics, could be defined in a nutshell—her husband John Jenkins.

So many times Nancy had heard testimonials from individuals who'd made wish lists and attested that the technique worked. Now she was living proof that dreams *can* come true by simply listing on paper your heart's desires and meditating over its existence in your life until, unconsciously, your destiny begins to unfold.

The once hopeless romantic doesn't regret marrying late in life, but Nancy does regret the time she wasted worrying and wondering if she'd ever find a husband and adds that if she could only turn back the hands of time, she would have spent her single years doing the exact same things she was doing when John Jenkins came along—taking trips with friends, playing golf and sailing on the weekends.

For years Nancy heard the old adage, *Life starts happening when you begin making other plans*, and now she avows to its truth because once she gave up hope and busied herself with outside activities, all her *Fairy Tale Fantasies* were fulfilled.

DIVINE INTERVENTION

FOR MONTHS, JEREMY CAMDEN, PASTOR of a Protestant church, contemplated asking out a member of his congregation. Fearing rejection, he had to muster up some courage because if Chelsea Chamberlain declined, a lot was at stake. For instance, Chelsea played a vital role in planning church activities, especially when it came to organizing events for the singles' group where she and Jeremy worked closely together. He, in no way, wished to create an uncomfortable situation for either of them. However, it seemed every time Jeremy turned around, he bumped into Chelsea. After a few unusual encounters, he wondered, *Is this fate or simply happenstance?*

While alone in his office one afternoon, he reflected on these unplanned engagements. It all started six months earlier when he transferred to a different parish. He would never forget leaving a town where he had grown up and driving two hundred miles to live in another city. Before he could unlock the door and unload his furniture in a house he'd soon call home, he first had to stop by the church office to pick up the key. Once he pulled into the parking lot, got out of his car and walked towards the rectory, the former pastor greeted him on the front steps. Not only did he welcome Jeremy, he also introduced him to the beautiful young woman he'd been talking to.

"Jeremy, meet Chelsea Chamberlain. She's going to be joining our church soon."

Thinking back, that beautiful young woman was the first person Jeremy met at his newly assigned parish.

Then Jeremy recalled the next time he saw Chelsea. How could he forget? The first Sunday he preached happened to be the day Chelsea joined the church. He felt honored to conduct the ceremony and formally initiated her into God's house.

Their encounters appeared inevitable, especially when the singles' group planned a one day hiking trip and the only two who showed up to go were he and Chelsea. While waiting an hour to see if others would arrive, they talked in-depth and came to know each other on a more personal level. Chelsea, a licensed psychologist, worked as an in-house counselor for a major corporation. She routinely exercised; and depending on the season, she enjoyed camping, hiking and snow-skiing. How ironic? So did Jeremy. After discovering they had so much in common, he wanted to ask Chelsea out so bad he couldn't stand it. With no crowd around, he'd been given the perfect opportunity. Still, he hesitated.

As these past events raced through Jeremy's memory, he called to mind *Three Boats and a Helicopter,* a tale he often told in his pastoral counseling to individuals seeking guidance. It is as follows: There once was a preacher that lived on the Louisiana Bayou. One day he received warning that a hurricane might hit, and law enforcement began evacuating the area. The preacher refused to leave home.

When the heavy rains came and flooded the streets, the preacher stood on his front porch and watched the water rise. A gentleman from the National Guard passed by in a boat. "Hey, Reverend, get in. I'll give you a ride and shelter."

"No," replied the preacher. "Just go on. God's watching out for me. I'll be fine."

The rain pounded harder and the flood waters rose above his front porch. Passengers in a second boat motored by. "Hey, Preacher, climb aboard. Let us give you a ride!"

He motioned for them to continue without him. "No, thank you. God's going to rescue me."

A state trooper passed in a third boat. "Hey, Preacher, you're going to drown. Jump on and I'll give you a ride."

"No. Thanks anyway, but God's going to save me. You'll see."

Finally, the flood waters rose above the first level. To avoid drowning, the preacher climbed onto the roof of his house. A helicopter flew overhead. The pilot landed on the roof and asked, "Preacher, can I give you a lift?"

"No," said the preacher, "I'm going to be a witness to millions! God's going to save me from drowning."

The flood waters rose above the rooftop and the minister drowned. When he entered heaven, he asked, "God, I was going to be a witness to millions. Why did you let me drown?"

God replied, "I tried! I sent you three boats and a helicopter."

After recalling this story, the joke seemed to be on Jeremy. In an instant, he realized the tale he often told to benefit others had now hit home. Just how many more chances would God give him before he would lose out?

Still alone in his office, Jeremy made the following request. "Okay, God. If you want me to ask Chelsea out, let her walk by my office."

There's no better verse to describe it than Matthew 7:7. "Ask, and you will be given what you ask for. Seek, and you will find. Knock, and the door will be opened."

The door was open, and no sooner did the pastor pray than he looked up and saw Chelsea passing by. To make certain his eyes were not deceiving him, Jeremy did a double-take. Once again, the story of *Three Boats and a Helicopter* flashed before him and he thought, *Lord, I cannot let this opportunity slip away.*

"Hey, Chelsea, come here for a minute!" he yelled.

Chelsea backed up and stood at his door. "I just wanted to know if you'd like to grab some dinner tonight?"

No question about it. Jeremy's invitation took Chelsea by surprise. She was simply on her way to Bible study. *When and where did that come from?* she wondered. With a startled look, she stated, "Well, yeah, but my meeting won't be over until 7:30."

"That's fine," Jeremy told her. "Just stop back by my office when you're done."

Jeremy couldn't believe it. He'd had many prayers answered in his life, but never one so immediate. In fact, he was half-kidding when he made his request. Obviously, God wasn't.

Meanwhile, Chelsea attended her meeting; and at 7:30, she met Jeremy in front of his office, her nerves a bit shaken. Of course Jeremy was no stranger to her, but then again, they'd only maintained a working relationship. Chelsea never expected to dine out with her minister.

Just this once I can go, she thought. Oddly enough, what Chelsea believed would be a one time thing actually resulted in a year of steady dating. They camped in the summer, hiked in the fall, and snow-skied in the winter.

At first the road to successful romance seemed smoothly paved; however, Jeremy had no way of foreseeing the potholes he'd face along his journey. It didn't take long for him to realize he loved Chelsea immensely and wanted to grow old with her. The loads of fun they had and the time they spent together proved them to be extremely compatible partners. Because Chelsea showered Jeremy with attention and affection, he felt confident she'd be honored to become his wife. But he got the surprise of his life when he proposed marriage.

"I could never marry a minister," she quickly informed him.

In her eyes, clergymen had to uphold a certain image,

one she felt she could never measure up to.

Another year of courtship and Jeremy had his work cut out for him. Aside from the congregation he ministered, he delivered sermons to Chelsea on a daily basis. *Preachers are human beings. Even though most people hold them to a higher standard, they're prone to make mistakes like everybody else. And they, too, experience the emotional highs and lows of life, just like everybody else. They're not perfect by any stretch of the imagination. You've got to understand this.*

Together, they managed to jump that hurdle. But right about the time Jeremy felt comfortable mentioning marriage again, Chelsea threw him another curve ball. Before engaging in a life-long commitment, she wanted to be certain of her feelings for Jeremy and insisted they date other people. Of course, after two years, Jeremy knew Chelsea well and had figured out her antics were merely excuses to avoid matrimony.

The truth of the matter lie hidden. Chelsea suffered from the common FOC Disease—Fear of Commitment. The "M" word horrified her. As far as she was concerned, marriage meant imprisonment, and she would go to all ends to escape it.

But having the faith of a minister and the patience of Job, Jeremy went along with Chelsea's suggestion, although he didn't like it. While he sat home alone, Chelsea played the field. In no time at all, she discovered other pastures weren't as green as the one she'd recently fled. Within two weeks, Chelsea returned to Jeremy, telling him it was strictly to date, not marry.

Like a trouper, Jeremy hung in there a third year. As long as they just dated and didn't speak of commitment, Chelsea could handle it. But right about the time she intuitively sensed the marriage subject might be up for discussion again, she pulled another caper. Her company had a job opening in a neighboring state, and Chelsea was willing to transfer. Jeremy wondered, *Why would a woman, who'd lived in the state of Virginia her entire life, develop a sudden desire to move to North Carolina?* Her reasoning this time: The 700 mile distance would certainly test the strength of their relationship. Chelsea even tried selling the idea to Jeremy. "Just think of all the hiking and camping we can do in the Blue Ridge Mountains when you *visit.*"

By now Jeremy had become well-schooled in dealing with a victim of the FOC Disease and understood that pushing or pressuring Chelsea to stay would only backfire. Instead of discouraging her wishes, he supported the concept by saying, "Well, sure. If that's what you really want to do, schedule an interview and see how North Carolina suits you."

Within a month, Chelsea boarded a plane and traveled to Charlotte, North Carolina. She was fired up about the job opening until she arrived for the interview. Everything that could go wrong did. First of all, the hiring supervisor made Chelsea wait two hours before conducting the interview. And there was absolutely no excuse for stalling because during that time, Chelsea could plainly see the supervisor was doing nothing but goofing off.

Sitting in a chair outside the woman's office, Chelsea couldn't help overhearing the woman's personal phone calls. She made arrangements for someone to walk her dog. After that conversation, she telephoned her hairdresser and scheduled a perm. Dozens of times, she traipsed back and forth to the break room for more coffee, never once offering Chelsea a cup.

Finally, after the supervisor handled everything job *unrelated,* she called Chelsea into her office. After observing this woman for two hours, Chelsea knew they'd never get along in a working environment; but since she'd traveled all that way at the company's expense, she felt obligated to complete the interview.

The situation seemed to go from bad to worse. Chelsea was stunned to discover there was no counseling position open. If offered the job, she'd be serving as secretary to this arrogant supervisor. To top it all off, the increase in salary she thought she would receive was barely enough to cover the cost of living. But if Chelsea had had a stick of dynamite when the supervisor asked her where she shopped for clothes and which sorority she was inducted into at college, she probably would have blown the woman up. *For crying out loud,* she thought, *what do name brand clothes and Greek-letter sororities have to do with job performance?*

Seeing this trip was a total waste of time, Chelsea politely slid her chair back, stood up, shook the supervisor's hand, thanked for her the interview, and said, "This job is not for me. I'll be excusing myself now."

The woman appeared stupefied, but Chelsea offered no explanation. Catching a taxi and crossing her fingers for the next departure, she couldn't get to the airport fast enough and arrived just in time to board the 4:00 p.m. flight. As the plane left the tarmac and soared thousands of feet in the air, Chelsea stared out the jet's window in silent meditation. Bombarding questions boggled her brain. *How much longer can I run? I know I love Jeremy and want to marry him, but I'm afraid. I've crawled through every escape hole I can find. How much more foolishness will he tolerate?*

As more agonizing thoughts flooded her memory, the story of *Three Boats and a Helicopter* struck a chord with Chelsea. *First, I told Jeremy I could never marry a minister. If that wasn't enough, I dated other people. Now I've tried to move 700 miles away from him. If I don't stop this nonsense, I'm going to lose the man I love. What am I going to do?*

As the jet rose above the clouds and reached cruising altitude, her answer came. While admiring the beautiful sun as it beamed brightly across the thick masses of fluffy clouds, Chelsea surrendered to the will of God. "Okay, Lord, I'm gonna do it."

What took three years to decide only took three months to plan. On a wintery white Christmas Eve morning, wedding bells rang for Jeremy and Chelsea in a small, historical church that overlooked a quiet and still lake.

After conquering her fear of commitment, Chelsea Chamberlain Camden shares her testimonial with victims suffering from the FOC Disease. "Ten years ago, marriage and motherhood were my greatest fears. Today, my husband and daughter are my most prized possessions. I didn't realize how miserable I was until I finally surrendered. The bottom line is: "It only works against us when we try to fight the will of God.""

And then there's her husband, Jeremy Camden, who deserves a big round of applause for three long years of perseverance. To hear his side of the story, "When I first met Chelsea, I felt there had to be a reason why I seemed to inevitably run into her; but when I sat at my desk and prayed, "Okay, God, if you want me to ask Chelsea out, let her walk by my office," and she did, why there was no doubt in my mind we were brought together through *Divine Intervention*.

"The three years we dated, I knew Chelsea was running scared and had tried every possible escape. It was basically a matter of time before she wore herself out. In the long run, it paid off. I can truly say: *Good things come to those who wait!*"

THE LAST LAUGH

MARY GRACE CASHIO AND HER sister, Angela, were running late for their cousin Donna's wedding. Since Angela would be a bridesmaid, their punctuality was important. Good old Mary Grace, known for her speedy foot, put the pedal to the metal in an effort to get to the church on time.

Their mother, Angel, was in the back seat hanging on for dear life as Mary Grace accelerated through yellow lights, passed in the turn lane, and dodged a few pedestrians. It was such a blessing they pulled into the church parking lot in one piece.

They rushed into the dressing room and found all the other bridesmaids scurrying around to finish last minute procedures. With forty-five minutes to go before the church bells would peal, everyone of them were emotional wrecks. Make-up had to be applied, hair still had to be styled, and a couple of dresses were yet to be pressed. Though Mary Grace was not in the wedding, she and her mother remained in the parlor and helped the bridesmaids tidy up.

During the hustle and bustle, in walked their cousin and sister of the bride, Rose Frances Burns. Because this woman of faith was best known for receiving phenomenal answers to her fervent prayers, friends and relatives frequently asked her to pray for them. To give one good example: Once she had a close friend whose husband was transferred to California. Because of the outrageous price of real estate, the family had trouble finding an affordable home. A devout Catholic, Rose Frances had studied the Bible intently, was well-rehearsed on all the Angels and Saints and could recite each and every role they played. So she advised her friend to ask St. Joseph, foster father of Jesus and finder of property, to help her locate a nice home. Meanwhile, Rose Frances prayed too. When her friend returned from shopping for a home in California, the first thing she did was telephone Rose Frances, "You're never going to believe this," she exclaimed. "We bought a home we never dreamed we could afford...on St. Joseph's Street."

So, now, with all the bridesmaids and relatives gathered in the Cathedral's parlor, and Rose Frances having their undivided attention, she started explaining why she claimed responsibility for her sister Donna's wedding, which was about to take place. The story she shared was so inspiring, the girls forgot their nervous jitters.

She told about one of the three Archangels, St. Raphael, whose story is derived from the *Book of Tobit* and is found in the Old Testament of the Catholic Bible; however, it was one of the seven books omitted from the King James Bible.

In the *Book of Tobit*, there was a woman named Sarah who was married seven times. Each time she married and her husband approached her for intercourse, he was killed by the wicked demon Asmodeus. The grief and insults Sarah received from the townspeople were more than she could bear, so she asked God to take her life, unless it was His will for her to live.

God heard Sarah's prayer for death and sent St. Raphael to instruct Tobiah, son of Tobit, to marry her. But Tobiah knew of Sarah's atrocities with husbands and objected to St. Raphael's instructions: "I have heard that this woman has already been married seven times, and that her husbands died in their bridal chambers. On the very night they approached her, they dropped dead. And I have heard it said that it was a demon who killed them. So now I too am afraid of this demon. Because he loves her, he does not harm her; but he does slay any man who wishes to come close to her. I am my father's only child. If I should die, I would bring my father and mother down to their grave in sorrow over me. And they have no other son to bury them." (*Tobit* 6:14–15).

St. Raphael replied, "So now listen to me, brother; do not give another thought to this demon, but marry Sarah. I know that tonight you shall have her for your wife. When you go into the bridal chamber, take the fish's liver and heart, and place them on the embers for the incense. As soon as the demon smells the odor they give off, he will flee and never again show himself near her. Then when you are about to have intercourse with her, both of you first rise up to pray. Beg the Lord of Heaven to show you mercy and grant you deliverance. But do not be afraid, for she was set apart for you before the world existed. You will save her, and she will go with you. And I suppose that you will have children by her, who will take the place of brothers for you. So do not worry." (*Tobit* 6:16–18).

Tobiah did fall deeply in love with Sarah and they married. After the wedding ceremony, Tobiah followed St. Raphael's instructions and placed the fish's liver and heart on the embers. When the demon smelled the incense, he fled and never returned.

Before making love that evening, Tobiah and Sarah arose from bed and asked for God's blessing and deliverance. After losing seven husbands to the wicked demon Asmodeus, Tobiah was the only husband Sarah had who lived; and, together, they had seven children. In Tobit 12:15, the Archangel reveals his identity. "I am Raphael, one of the seven angels who enter and serve before the Glory of the Lord."

Once Rose Frances finished sharing St. Raphael's role in the *Book of Tobit* and explained why she claimed responsibility for her sister Donna's wedding, every bridesmaid stood in awe. Still congregated in the Cathedral's parlor, Rose Frances Burns expounded upon the fact that since St. Raphael was the Archangel of love, she'd many times asked God in prayer to send St. Raphael to find a good Christian husband for single women she knew. Miraculously, within a few weeks or months from the time she prayed, that particular girl would have met a remarkable man and eventually married him.

To prove this technique had worked, she named all the girls she prayed for who had married soon afterwards. As a matter of fact, just weeks after Rose Frances prayed for her sister Donna to find a husband, it seemed Donna's fiancé, Richard, appeared from the middle of nowhere, and now their wedding ceremony was only minutes away.

By this time, not only were the bridesmaids mouths hanging open, their pupils had expanded to twice their normal size. The unmarried women felt they'd found a savior in Rose Frances Burns and immediately begged her to pray for them too. That's when Mary Grace's mother, Angel, who'd also been listening intently, intervened. "Rose Frances, I don't mean don't pray for these other girls, but if you're going to pray for anybody, please pray for my daughter Mary Grace. She's a single mother, raising a child all by herself. She needs some help, and that little girl needs a father."

Sad, but true. Mary Grace married at a young age and later divorced. The only valuable thing she left with was her daughter Jessica. Resembling a porcelain doll, the seven year old drew a crowd everywhere she went. Most girls would give anything to have her olive skin that blended beautifully with the child's long and thick, brown hair and lustrous brown eyes.

Everything shined on the outside, but no one could see the darkness within. Jessica's biological father would promise her all the fun and excitement a child could imagine before his weekend visitation. On Friday afternoons when he was due to pick her up, Jessica would sit on their front porch, her little suitcase by her side, and wait for him to pull into the driveway. Hours passed. Her father would neither come, nor call. After his countless no-shows and broken promises, Jessica gave up hope on seeing her dad.

Angel Cashio had good intentions for her daughter and granddaughter when she asked Rose Frances Burns to pray for Mary Grace to find a husband. And, of course, Mary Grace appreciated her mother's concerns; but after fighting a bitter divorce, she wasn't the least bit convinced about this St. Raphael stuff. It humored her. Mary Grace could laugh all she wanted, but Rose Frances took this matter seriously; and because every woman she'd prayed for had a successful marriage soon afterwards, she had every reason to believe it would work for Mary Grace also.

The big moment was about to arrive. Outside the sanctuary, the attendants lined the hall to make their debut down the aisle. As they reached final countdown and the Wedding March began to play, the single bridesmaids reminded Rose Frances, "Don't forget to pray for us unweds to find a husband."

Mary Grace, who was now helping direct Donna's wedding, chuckled, "Yeah, Rose Frances, bet I'll be next!"

The ceremony went off without a hitch. Donna and Richard became husband and wife. For everyone else, life resumed to normal.

The following Monday, Mary Grace returned to her job as a customer representative for a specialty wine and gift shop. Over the course of that next month, business became a little different than the norm. A flurry of men started coming around like never before. Suddenly it seemed like their only customers were male, chatting flirtatiously with the dark-haired, dark-eyed, vivacious Italian. There was no question about it, Mary Grace liked all the attention. Even her boss, a good-natured kind of guy, couldn't help but notice that there had definitely been a drastic change in business and commented, "For goodness sakes, Mary Grace! What in the Sam Hill is going on around this place? I'm trying to run a business, and it seems lately you're entertaining every guy in town."

Kiddingly, she told him this barrage of men was probably a result of her cousin Rose Frances's prayer for her to find a husband. "Well," he said, "my wife's got a fella she wants to introduce you to....if you're interested."

Because Mary Grace had such a tough time with her ex-husband, she could have cared less about meeting someone new. "Well, I'm not ready to date just yet, but I'll keep that in mind when I am," she told her boss.

It seemed if guys weren't stopping by the store where Mary Grace worked, they were calling her on the phone, especially Charlie Rizzo. She'd known him for years. In fact, they graduated from high school together. Like clockwork, everyday at noon, Charlie telephoned Mary Grace because he knew she would be in the shop alone. Though he was single also, their relationship was strictly platonic. After Mary Grace divorced, the two had a standing joke. *Yeah, if we don't find someone decent by the time we're 60, we'll just marry each other.*

Well, one February day, just two months after Rose Frances promised to pray for all the single women at her sister Donna's wedding, Mary Grace was in the store alone. The lunch hour was slow and she was bored. She thought, *Well, it's noon. Charlie should be calling any minute now.* About that time, the phone rang.

A deep, sexy voice asked, "May I speak to Mary Grace?" Immediately she wondered, *What on earth is*

Charlie doing asking for me when he knows it's me he's talking to? Well, she thought, *two can play this game. I'll fix him. I'll throw him a line that will leave him speechless.* And with that she certainly did. "Hey, baby, are you gonna come over and jump in the cooler with me and let me have my way with you?"

There was a long pause. Then you could hear..."Aha... Aha...ha...ha...ha! You must not know who this is," said the caller.

And, obviously, she didn't. Mary Grace only knew who it *wasn't.* Her face blushed as she hung up the phone and buried her head into her hands, all the while hoping whoever wouldn't call back. But he did. Mary Grace said she would rather eat a worm than answer the phone, yet she had no choice; she was the only one there. No doubt it was the same guy because when Mary Grace answered the second time, he was still laughing and even asked, "Mary Grace, what was that comment? You want to do....What? When? Where?"

Realizing there was no escape, Mary Grace decided, *What the heck! I'll just blow this off. I mean, what more of a fool could I make of myself today?* Besides, by the way this guy laughed and persisted, it didn't appear Mary Grace was getting rid of him anytime soon.

Finally she asked, "Okay. Who is this?"

"Well, I'm David Kaufmann. I'm in the advertising business, and I spoke to the manager of your company earlier about ordering a ham to give to one of my customers."

Mary Grace took a deep breath. Once she recovered from her professional faux pas, she said, "We've got it ready. Do you want us to deliver it or are you going to come in and pick it up?"

Actually, David planned on having the ham delivered. But after speaking with Mary Grace, the human ham that suggested jumping in the cooler, he decided to drive to the gift shop and pick it up himself. Why not? David was a sexy single, curious to see for himself if Mary Grace's looks were as pleasing as her personality.

However, before David could get there, Mary Grace's boss returned from lunch. In a state of hysterics, she told him about the audacious comment she thought she'd made to Charlie Rizzo and what resulted when she discovered it was a customer calling to inquire about a ham. Because her supervisor had taken the order for the ham earlier that morning, he asked, "That wouldn't happen to have been David Kaufmann, would it?"

"Yes," she replied. "It certainly was."

"You're kidding! That's the fella my wife wants you to meet."

Twenty minutes later, David Kaufmann walked into the wine and gift shop. There stood Mary Grace behind the front counter. Of course, after they formally introduced themselves, David began teasing Mary Grace about her daring suggestion to "jump in the cooler." But once he decided to put a lid on the "cooler" subject and continued talking about things in general, their conversation moved into high gear. A stranger would have thought he and Mary Grace had known each other a lifetime. With so much to say in such a short amount of time, they had to stop themselves from talking over each other. Because their encounter went so well and seemed promising, David invited Mary Grace to play racquetball with him that evening.

"Sure. I love to play racquetball," she replied.

So that night the two of them met at a local sports club. Without a doubt, it was one heck of a game. See, Mary Grace was not being one hundred percent honest when she told David she loved to play racquetball, but she wasn't about to miss the chance to go on a date with this man. In all candor, Mary Grace had never played racquetball in her life. The truth told on her when she pivoted right to return a shot that wasn't hers to return. At the exact same time, David was following through on a forward swing. It was too late for any last minute warning. The strength of this 6'4" brown-haired, blue-eyed husky caused Mary Grace a concussion and two bruised knees. And this was just the beginning of their courtship. Although Mary Grace wasn't good at the sport, she was a *good sport* when she refused to let defeat or embarrassment stand in the way of a budding romance.

Evidently, Rose Frances's prayer had been heard. By the way things were happening, it appeared God had once again summoned St. Raphael to the rescue. And the Archangel was doing an outstanding job of finding Mary Grace a good man. Within no time, David grew to love Jessica as if she were his own. He coached her softball team, met her teachers, and even carried her on dates with he and Mary Grace. All the love David gave, Jessica returned. For he was the father she needed and dreamed of having.

And on June 25th, 1988, at David and Mary Grace's wedding, Jessica let God and the congregation know how thankful she was. Dressed in a white satin and lace dress, a blue sash tied around her waist, and shiny white ballet shoes, this grateful seven year old walked confidently to the altar after David and Mary Grace exchanged vows. All eyes were on her. You could hear the whispers of curious people throughout, "What is she about to do?"

The priest adjusted the microphone to reach her tiny lips and held a picture she'd drawn of a man, woman and child standing in a field of flowers. In a loud, clear voice, she read a poem that stole the hearts of the congregation:

> *Here I am a little girl, calling you God to have a word.*
>
> *It's all about my new friend David. He makes me laugh.*

He makes me smile. He never, ever makes me mad
He loves my mom and he loves me, and I'm so
glad that we'll be three. So I thank you
God for giving
David to me.

Afterwards, there wasn't a dry eye in the house. One lady was sobbing so uncontrollably, she excused herself from the sanctuary.

It's been nine years since that monumental moment, and it's no longer "I'm so glad that we'll be three." Since June 25th, 1988, the date they tied the knot, God blessed David, Mary Grace and Jessica with Katie, Joe, and Bryan.

It's funny how what goes around usually comes around. When Rose Frances told the St. Raphael story to all the bridesmaids at her sister Donna's wedding and promised to pray for them to find a good husband, Mary Grace was the skeptic that chuckled. But in the end, while sitting in attendance at David and Mary Grace's wedding, it was Rose Frances Burns who got *The Last Laugh!*

BEATING THE STREETS

ILEARNED A LONG TIME AGO not to question the mind of God. But I'll admit, I was having a difficult time understanding my life at the present and was quickly losing patience with the Lord. I thought by accepting a job in Alabama and leaving Florida, I was avoiding financial breakdown and obeying God's command. But even after being in an entirely different state for four months and, still, nothing in my life was going right, I began to wonder if I had misread the signs. Instead of hitting the bottom of the barrel, I slammed through it going full speed, and there seemed to be no end in sight.

For instance, one day I was walking through Birmingham's business district to get back to my office when, in the blink of an eye, I looked up and discovered a street drunk approaching me with an empty whiskey bottle. He had it rared back in his hand and was about to whop me upside the head with it. As I ducked to avoid an unnecessary blow, he appeared terribly frightened, as if he'd just seen a ghost. Instead of busting my noggin with the bottle, he quickly threw it in the trash and fled.

I glanced over my left shoulder to see what angel had rescued me *this time*, and there was literally a policeman on a white horse. He jumped off, chased the guy down the sidewalk, placed him in handcuffs, then radioed for a cruiser to pick the guy up and take him to jail.

Aside from that ordeal, I had more than my share of financial difficulties. More than once I was instructed, well in advance, what time to report to a deposition; however, at the last minute, when I had no possible way of making it across town within a reasonable hour in heavy traffic, my office would inform me that the time of deposition changed and they sent someone else to cover the job. On a different occasion, the incorrect street address and building were written on my notice of deposition. After being lost for fifteen minutes, I stopped at a convenience store and called for accurate directions.

By the time I arrived, I was in such a hurry to assemble my court reporting machine, I bent over wrong and my back popped out of place. So while I'm stenographically reporting this witness being grilled by a lawyer about his back injury, I'm sitting there suffering excruciating pain with mine. For the next three weeks, I was physically unable to work. Once I recovered and was able to report, there was no work.

Being an independent contractor, I could do outside jobs. So I tried to make money as a medical transcriptionist, until disaster struck with that. Before this, I'd never, in my entire working career, received insufficient funds from anyone. Trying to collect pay from this *"no-dough"* was bad enough; but when I returned to the individual's office to ask for cash, I got more than I bargained for. The pay-er had the audacity to look me in the eye and say, "Well, if you don't have the money in your account, the bank won't cash the check."

After hearing that remark, I'm grateful I wasn't permanently stuck with the facial expression I made. I wanted to counterattack by saying, "No, you're confused. The bank won't cash the check if you, the pay-er, don't have the money in your account," but I figured what the heck. It would have fallen on deaf ears. Eventually, I got paid; but I had to hang around their office on a daily basis and beg for the few hundred bucks I was owed.

After that experience, I took a few days off from court reporting and medical transcription and volunteered to babysit, hoping my luck would change. While driving down Interstate 65-South, on my way to keep this child, I noticed something in the road. *Oh, my Lord!* I screamed as I swerved to avoid it. Minutes later, *Poooofff.* Thank God I made it to the gas station with a flat. My last $85 paid for the new tire.

By the middle of June, I threw my hands in the air and accepted the fact that the rest of my life might be sewage. Instead of admitting myself into an insane asylum, I did what any self-supporting American would only dare: I quit my job.

My banker knew me personally and was up-to-date on my recent trials and tribulations. I went to him in desperation. As crazy as it may sound to some, I told him that I truly felt like God wanted me to work on this book, and court reporting, along with everything else, was causing too many distractions. Nothing seemed to be in my favor but *Marriages Meant To Be.* My efforts to make a living had failed, yet I could walk into a bathroom or a restaurant and collect an unusual marriage story.

As I continued my unending saga, the banker nodded his head as though he'd traveled that same path a time or two; and without any further discussion, he loaned me enough money to live on through the summer months.

With a replenished bank account and a sense of relief, I wasted no time beating the streets in search of stories. I thought bridal shops would be an excellent place to start so I drove to a store where I knew the people were friendly. I'd had some fliers printed, and I asked the manager, Sheree, if I could hang a few on their bulletin board. She seemed interested and quizzed me about the type stories I was seeking. After I shared a few, she looked at me and said, "You've got to get my parents story. In fact, in 1979, William Bradford Huie wrote a book about my father titled *It's Me O Lord,* and my parents marriage story is in there. Believe me, it's a marriage made in heaven," she said.

After hearing it, I agreed with Sheree. Her parents marriage *was* meant to be.

A DREAM COME TRUE

BECOMING A PREACHER WAS THE last thing Dan Ronsisvalle thought of doing. He had better things going for him, or so he thought. This gorgeous Italian was not only the star player on his high school football team, he had the privilege of being every girls' heartthrob. Besides, he'd had his fill with ministers.

For instance, Dan and his sisters, Ruth, Jo and Sara, had a talent for singing and called themselves *The Italian Gospel Trio*. While traveling around the country and performing in various churches, Dan became thoroughly disgusted once when he discovered a preacher gazing through a peephole outside the womens' dressing room. There was no doubt in Dan's mind the minister enjoyed watching the girls change from choir robes to regular clothes.

But Dan really seemed to lose faith in clergymen when some members at one congregation informed him a few preachers had cheated them on the offering. In an effort to inspire people while struggling to survive, *The Italian Gospel Trio* received far less pay than the amount accounted for in the collection plate. He found it hard to believe the people of the church would dare to take advantage.

But with age came wisdom. Soon Dan realized it's not the title that makes the difference; it's the person. Knowing he'd been blessed with the ability to touch the lives of others, Dan Ronsisvalle traveled to Waxahachie, Texas and enrolled at Southwestern Bible College in September 1955.

Was he ever grateful he'd accepted his calling into the ministry! Once Violet Fern Tidwell, the beautiful brown-eyed brunette, took his hand and welcomed him as a freshman, Dan knew instantly God intended for this woman to one day become his bride.

He hung around the school's entrance and patiently waited for a chance to talk to Fern Tidwell. Just as the crowd cleared, he approached the woman he'd yet to take his eyes off of. "Would you like to join me for ice cream in the soda shop?" he asked.

Evidently, Dan was going to need a cold treat to cool him off because when Fern responded, "Sure, I would," he nearly melted.

While talking in the school's snack shop, Dan discovered Fern had many unique qualities. For example, she was no newcomer around the campus. At a mature fifteen, Fern left home and entered tenth grade at Southwestern's high school. Actively involved with church and youth groups most of her life, Fern even received an exhorter's permit in the spring of 1950, which allowed her to stand in the pulpit of any Assemblies of God in her district and minister for the Lord.

Through the years, she had established a wonderful relationship with God. Now, at the age of twenty, Fern hoped to find her special someone and eventually marry; however, before doing so, her future husband had to meet certain criteria. First, he must understand that the right Christian marriage should be based on deep affection, complete honesty, and the mutual belief that marriages are made in heaven and should last until death. He couldn't be an egotistical type nor a male chauvinist. Fern preferred to marry a male minister who would accept the fact that she, too, was an effective minister.

But more importantly, she believed no one should rush into a relationship and should be extremely meticulous when selecting a spouse, and that choosing the right partner begins with asking for God's help in finding the right Christian mate.

Through the eyes of Dan Ronsisvalle, Fern Tidwell was the most sensational lady he'd met and probably would ever know. From the moment he first saw her, Dan became enthralled with Fern's good looks and gentle handshake; but after sitting down and having a conversation with her, he was blinded by her beauty and became overwhelmingly impressed with her intelligence and dedication to Christ.

Stirred even more, Dan couldn't wait to ask her for a dinner date; but had he known she would refuse, he might not have been so anxious. In a short amount of time, Dan quickly learned that serving God was Fern's number one priority, and although she had acquired many male friends at Southwestern, Fern was careful not to let too many dating distractions interfere with her service to the Lord.

Besides, Fern had enough faith in God to know that if Dan Ronsisvalle was the man He had chosen for her to marry, then the Lord would let her know in more ways than one. Until then, she would hold out for the signals.

On the other hand, Dan Ronsisvalle had certainly seen brighter days. No woman had ever turned him down before, so rejection was something he didn't quite know how to handle. Trying to figure out how to win Fern Tidwell's heart had him scrambling for clues.

However, luck was on his side when he introduced himself to a classmate named Bobby. When Dan pronounced his last name—Ronsisvalle—Bobby recognized it and asked, "Hey, did you ever have relatives in the service? I went through basic training at Fort Hood, Texas with a guy by the name of Joe Ronsisvalle."

"Joe Ronsisvalle?" Dan exclaimed. "Why that's my older brother."

What a small world! Bobby went even further, "Yeah,

we were buddies through boot camp. We went to church together. I really liked your brother and always wanted him to meet my younger sister."

Well, it was too late to introduce Joe Ronsisvalle to any woman. He had already married, and it was a good thing because Bobby's younger sister happened to be Violet Fern Tidwell.

At the time, Bobby didn't know it, but he'd just done the greatest favor he'd probably ever done for anybody; and Dan thanked God for opening an avenue. "I really would like a date with your sister. Do you think you might could help me out?"

It never hurts to ask. Bobby Tidwell let Dan know he'd be delighted to put in a good word. Apparently, older brother followed through on his promise because Fern reconsidered; and that Friday night, she and Dan attended chapel together. Afterwards, they spent hours talking.

Over the next few months, every weekend turned into the same ritual; after attending chapel, Dan and Fern hung around the campus and wound up talking for hours upon end. Occasionally, when Dan could afford it, they would drive to Dallas and dine at an upscale restaurant.

Aside from Fern falling in love, Dan Ronsisvalle had achieved something far greater than the other guys she'd dated: It appeared he met all Fern's requirements for being a wonderful Christian husband because after lengthy discussions regarding marriage, the ministry, and raising children, Fern confided to Dan one of her major concerns, "I have a divine calling upon my life. I have a ministry I can never ignore. So if we are married, I'll have to be faithful to my calling, and you'll have to respect my calling."

Of course, Dan Ronsisvalle had no problem with that. As a matter of fact, he knew, together, they would make a great evangelistic team. By February of 1956, Fern agreed to marry Dan. Yet before she would follow through with a wedding ceremony, she wanted him to travel to West Monroe, Louisiana and meet her family.

Astonishingly enough, once Fern became engaged, an interesting thing happened to confirm the fact that Dan *was* the man God had chosen for her. About a week before journeying to her hometown, Fern had flashbacks of a long forgotten dream that stemmed from a frightening experience she had as a little girl. When Fern was only ten years old, she had attended a youth crusade in West Monroe, Louisiana. That evening, the preacher shared a story about a young woman whose fiancé pretended to be a fine Christian; but once they married, the man forbid his wife to attend church. Because of his violence and cruelty, they later divorced. The woman's story had such a profound effect on Fern, that before going to sleep that night, she knelt down beside her bed and prayed, "Oh, Lord, please don't ever let anything like that happen to me."

Once Fern quieted down and fell asleep, she dreamed that she was much older, lived away from home, and was dating a minister who had dark, wavy hair. In Fern's dream, the preacher had several sisters, a short first name and a long difficult last name, and she was engaged to him before he met her parents for the first time. Because the dream was so vivid and real, Fern talked about it to many different people, particularly her family.

If it wasn't enough that the dark-haired minister in Fern's dream had a short first name and a long, difficult last name, plus several sisters, D-A-N R-O-N-S-I-S-V-A-L-L-E, the man Fern was engaged to, not only preached, but actually had black, wavy hair and seven sisters.

Why, a week before Fern was to introduce Dan to her family, had she suddenly retrieved a dream that had been obscured from her memory for over a decade? "For God speaks again and again, in dreams, in visions of the night when deep sleep falls on men as they lie on their beds." (*Job* 33:14-15).

Fern told no one, but prayed that if the dream she had at the age of ten were truly prophetic and Dan Ronsisvalle was the man God had chosen for her to marry, that two other people would recall the dream also.

One week later, with places to go, things to do, and people to see, Dan and Fern threw their luggage in the trunk of the car and took off for West Monroe. Not only would Dan Ronsisvalle meet the entire Tidwell family, that evening he planned to preach in the church where Fern was raised. After he delivered a dynamic sermon, Fern's mother approached her; and out of the clear blue, she shouted, "Do you remember that dream you had when you were a little girl? Well, this is the one. This is the man you're supposed to marry!"

Almost simultaneously, Fern's Aunt Rita walked over and exclaimed, "He's the one. That's the man from your dream."

As far as seeking guidance on whether Dan was the right partner, Fern's prayer had been answered in the exact manner she requested. And on June 8th, 1956, less than a year from the date they met, Dan and Fern Ronsisvalle married.

"What God hath joined together, let no man put asunder." Their faith and love of the Lord, service and dedication to Him, plus over forty great years together and the raising of two children all speaks for itself. Dan and Fern Ronsisvalle's marriage *was* made in heaven and more than a *Dream Come True*.

THE JOLLY GREEN JETTA

AFTER TWO YEARS OF RIGOROUS studying, Clarissa Hayes finally entered her last semester at Duke University. But in order to graduate a licensed physical therapist, she was required to complete fifteen weeks of affiliations in a medical facility. The college gave students a choice by supplying a list of numerous hospitals in metropolitan areas where internships could be performed; and from that sheet, residents were allowed to select two cities where they wished to intern. If perhaps their first selection wasn't available, they automatically received their second option.

Out of the fifty states, Clarissa chose Colorado. Because she received her undergraduate at the University of Boulder and had many friends there, it only made sense that she return. But if the truth be known, that wasn't the only reason. Clarissa had an old flame living in St. Louis. In her mind, she had it all planned out. If she were lucky enough to land Boulder, that would mean she would travel through Missouri to get there. She'd always remember her first love...and with good reason. Why, before they met at the fresh age of eighteen, Clarissa had never even been kissed by another fellow, so when his lips touched hers for the first time, it's no wonder Clarissa went absolutely *goo goo* over the young man. Since they had broken up, she longed for his tender love and affection. Gosh, she thought, if their five year relationship could be as wonderful as it once was, then visions of a romantic reunion filled her heart with hope.

Becoming so wrapped up in sweet memories, Clarissa seemed to forget why she and her armor parted ways. In the beginning of their courtship everything was hunky dory, but after three years of dating, the relationship began to deteriorate and he became nothing more than a hard habit to break.

Subconsciously, Clarissa knew better than to try and rekindle sparks with her old flame, but something about good-bye forever had a strange psychological effect. Instead of focusing on reasons for good riddance, Clarissa dwelled on their most treasured times together, which made letting go of the past awfully hard to do.

Luckily, the dilemma resolved itself when Clarissa received a letter from the school stating Boulder wasn't available. It was just as well because she needed to branch out into a different area and become more independent.

Instead of transferring to a familiar place, Clarissa had no choice but to load up and leave for a city she'd never even visited. Widely known for their outstanding medical facilities, she had selected Birmingham, Alabama as a second option. Though a little disappointed Boulder didn't work out, she welcomed change and accepted this as an omen...*Maybe I don't belong with my old flame. Perhaps better plans lay elsewhere!*

With her Honda Accord packed solid, she left the Carolina Mountains and headed for new life in Alabama. Before beginning affiliations, she had a week to sight-see and become acquainted with the area, but that still didn't cure her blues. On a crisp and cool Sunday in January 1991, Clarissa decided to take an afternoon stroll through a nearby park. There, amongst the peace and beauty of nature, she could draw upon her Higher Power for strength and the courage to carry on emotionally.

Sitting on a park bench under a large oak tree, Clarissa, lost and lonely, cried out to God in prayer. *Dear Lord,*

I'm so alone here. My friends are scattered about. My family is in California. If anything happened to me, nobody would ever know it. I'm afraid I'll never get married and nobody will ever love me. Please rid me of these gut-wrenching feelings and let me be happy just being Clarissa Hayes. AMEN!

Suddenly, the sun shone so brightly in her face, she couldn't help but believe that was the Lord's way of giving her His peace. With more enthusiasm than ever, Clarissa walked home and prepared herself for the busy week ahead.

After counting down the days for work to begin, Monday finally rolled around. Thank goodness! Clarissa couldn't wait to meet new people! To start the day off right, she woke up early and left home in plenty of time to beat the traffic. The designated parking lot that adjoined the hospital was mostly empty. Wanting a sense of security, Clarissa parked beside a shiny, green Volkswagen Jetta. At first, she thought nothing about it. The Jetta was basically the car she parked next to, but an unusual occurrence piqued her curiosity. Everyday for the next three weeks, that shiny, green Volkswagen Jetta was parked in the same space. When Clarissa would leave work at 5:00 p.m., the car was always gone.

She would be the first to admit she's no visionary; but for some unknown reason, Clarissa was drawn to this particular vehicle and felt compelled to seek out the driver. Because a fraternity sticker hung in the center of the vehicle's back window, she could only assume the owner must be male.

On several occasions, she arrived for work an hour early hoping to spot the driver of the car, but to no avail. The Jetta would be sitting in the parking lot, but the owner was nowhere to be found. *Maddening!* Clarissa couldn't figure out what frustrated her the most: The strange fact that the car was parked in the same spot every day, or her unsuccessful attempts to locate its owner.

After three weeks of nearly going insane, Clarissa gathered her nerve. Ready to take on a challenge, she pulled a napkin from her glove compartment and wrote, "Happy Friday, from the California Honda." When no one was watching, she placed it on the windshield of the Jetta.

As usual, when Clarissa left work that afternoon, the Jetta was gone. However, the napkin lay under her left windshield wiper with a handwritten response, "Happy Friday to you, Hugh."

Oh, boy! Clarissa had stirred up some excitement. So filled with jubilation, she even looked forward to work the following Monday. And she should have because that afternoon she received another note from Hugh. This time he asked, "Do you always leave notes on the vehicles you park beside?"

As far as looks, Hugh could have been the creature from the black lagoon, but that didn't seem to matter. Clarissa appreciated his humor and decided she would continue corresponding. But by the time she got the note, his Jetta was gone, so she had to wait until the following day to respond. The next morning Clarissa answered Hugh's question, "Only cute green Jettas!"

For the next few days, they passed notes via their vehicles. Clarissa explained she was in her last semester at Duke and her job in Birmingham was only temporary. Hugh wrote and told her he was in his first year of medical school.

Because she could only locate the car and never the mystery man that drove it, Clarissa asked Hugh if he worked nights at the hospital. "No," he wrote. "I hustle to work extra early each morning to beat rush-hour traffic."

Finally, a logical explanation as to why her spying

techniques had failed.

Then one morning Clarissa panicked as she entered the parking lot. *Could the man peering through the windshield of the Jetta be Hugh?* she wondered. *Oh, gosh, I'm not ready for this.* Instead of driving up and introducing herself, she peeled off. For the next ten minutes, Clarissa rode through a residential area hoping the guy would be gone when she returned. After all, she had to report to work.

Hallelujah! When she crept back into the parking lot, the guy had disappeared. Afraid of getting caught, Clarissa got out of her car, walked passed the Jetta as though it didn't exist, and hurried inside the hospital.

Boy, did she feel like an idiot! Not only did she feel like one, but the people she worked with declared her mentally deranged. Being a native Californian, best known as the land of the fruits and nuts, didn't boost their opinion of her. Leaving notes on a stranger's vehicle was unheard of in Birmingham, Alabama.

Funny how Clarissa didn't care what anyone thought. She had a sensational feeling about this man and she wasn't about to let any straight-laced folks spoil her good time.

Later that afternoon, a co-worker came in from lunch and told Clarissa, "You should see what he left for you today!"

In a flash, Clarissa vanished. Seconds later she surfaced in the parking lot. While peeking inside the Jetta, Clarissa became engrossly captivated with what she discovered. *Good grief,* she thought, *I haven't even met this guy and look how thoughtful he is.*

Through correspondence, Clarissa mentioned missing her family. After learning she was a California native and knowing she was homesick, Hugh thought it might brighten her spirits if he brought a collage of pictures he took while visiting there and placed them on the inside of his windshield for her viewing. Clarissa couldn't believe it. The pictures were of places all too familiar. Hugh had vacationed just a few miles down the road from where she grew up.

After putting in a full day's work, Clarissa left the hospital. Once she exited the building and stepped into the parking lot, she saw that same guy who'd been peering through the windshield of the Jetta earlier that morning, only now he was wearing an orange vest. Whew! Was she relieved to discover the individual she thought was Hugh turned out to be a security guard just getting a glimpse of the collage of pictures Hugh had propped on the dashboard.

By this time, it seemed Clarissa was on a first name basis with every male employee at her place of work. The only man she had not yet encountered was Hugh. Since her job in Birmingham was only temporary, she feared time was ticking away, and she would return to Duke having never met her mystery man.

Fortunately, after nine exciting days of note writing, Hugh did finally ask Clarissa for her number; but once again, by the time she got to her car, he'd already left work. To avoid missing him a second time, she wrote her phone number down the next day, ran out to the parking lot on her lunch hour and placed the note on his windshield. That evening Hugh called. Ten days of written correspondence and a two hour conversation that evening proved they had something to talk about. Instead of chatting on the phone all night, they decided to continue their conversation over lunch the next day. Clarissa was so ecstatic she could hardly sleep!

February 13th, 1991…her day to meet the mystery man finally arrived! In a restaurant on Birmingham's Southside, Clarissa and Hugh formally introduced themselves. *Um…um…um, if Hugh Sharp wasn't the stuff!* The six foot bronze tanned, muscle man had brown hair, and blue eyes that mesmerized. Of course, Hugh didn't look as though he wished to run the other way when he saw Clarissa. He confessed later that she was as cute as the notes she had written. Tall, thin, blond hair, blue eyes, and charming dimples he couldn't resist.

There's no doubt Clarissa liked what she saw, and she hoped lunch was just the preamble to what lay ahead. While eating, they cracked jokes about their ten days of note writing, and Hugh asked, "So whatever prompted you to leave a note on my car?"

"Oh, well," Clarissa told him, "Because it was my first day on the job and I was scared, I needed a sense of security. And the Jetta looked so inviting, I just pulled in beside it. But seeing that car parked in the same spot three weeks in a row fascinated me, and I thought I would lose my mind if I didn't find out who drove that vehicle."

Hugh seemed quite impressed. "Well, no woman has ever approached me in that manner; but I have to be honest, I think it's pretty neat. It tells me you're adventuresome, and I like that."

After an hour, they both had to end their conversation and return to work. Before they left, Hugh turned to her and said, "I'll call you later."

"Later?" Gosh, she wondered, *later* sounds vague. That could mean tonight, tomorrow, or two weeks, if ever. Through her dating experiences, Clarissa learned many things, but the most important lesson was this: Never sit home and wait for the phone to ring. Instead, she met a girlfriend for dinner and didn't get in until ten o'clock.

If Clarissa had stayed home and waited for Hugh to call, he probably wouldn't have, but her strong-will and determination paid off because when she played her messages back, nothing thrilled her more than: "This is Hugh! Just thought I'd call and see what you were up to. Give me a call me when you get in."

Cupid couldn't have struck at a more perfect time. Since the next day was Valentine's, Clarissa planned to bake Hugh some homemade cookies...but only if he telephoned. Of course, if he didn't, he wouldn't be lucky enough to even get a card. First she returned his call, and because their conversation lasted two hours, Hugh would definitely get the pleasure of tasting her mouth-melting Chocolate Chip Cookies. When they hung up the phone at the stroke of midnight, Clarissa made a mad dash to the grocery store to purchase the secret ingredients and stayed up half the night baking them.

And on St. Valentine's Day, when Clarissa handed Hugh a fresh batch of cookies, he presented her with a *Will You Be Mine* card. Throughout the remaining weeks of Clarissa's residency, she and Hugh didn't miss one day of seeing each other. Having so much faith in this relationship, Clarissa informed her family on March 2nd, just three weeks after meeting Hugh, that she had met the man she was going to marry; though he hadn't realized it yet, soon he would.

Before accepting full-time employment that would make Birmingham a permanent home, Clarissa returned to Duke University in the spring of that same year, 1991, and graduated with honors. Afterwards, she returned to Birmingham; and throughout the summer, she and Hugh enjoyed camping, biking, and beach going. Seven months was all it took to convince them they were no good without each other.

On August 2nd, 1991, high atop Monte-sano Mountain in Huntsville, Alabama, Hugh proposed. And the prediction Clarissa so confidently made to her family came true on March 21st, 1992, when, just thirteen months after they met, she and Hugh married.

Before coming to Alabama, Clarissa walked down memory lane and wondered why the relationship between she and her old flame never worked out; and why had she received her second option—Birmingham—over her first choice—Boulder. And once she arrived for her first day of affiliations and continuing three weeks later, what was it about that shiny, green Jetta that forced her to leave a note on the car in an attempt to find the owner?

When all was said and done, the pieces of the puzzle were gathered and put in their proper places. A perfect picture formed and Clarissa could plainly see why the relationship between she and her old flame fizzled. A blessing in disguise! Traveling to Birmingham was all part of the plan. And the overwhelming compulsion she had to locate the owner of the Jetta happened to be the key that unlocked the door to her destiny.

Clarissa is more than thankful Boulder didn't work out and is forever grateful she traveled to Birmingham to complete her residency. As far as those certain co-workers that labeled her a nutcase…Well, they learned something valuable from Clarissa's experience: *Nothing ventured, nothing gained.*

Smiling, she and Hugh gracefully sum it up, "We believe we have one of the best relationships in the world. We have a lot of fun together, are best friends as well as lovers, and both understand the importance of family and our relationship. We thank our lucky stars for putting us in the right spot at the right time. Our meeting had to be from God. When something you want so desperately doesn't work out, it only means something better is around the corner."

And for Clarissa, it was not just the *Jolly Green Jetta* parked around the corner, but most importantly, the owner of that car, her husband, Hugh Sharp.

GOOD LOOKS WAS ALL IT TOOK

"**D**OROTHY, SOME DAY YOUR KNIGHT is going to come riding through on a white horse and sweep you right off of your feet." When twenty year old Dorothy Jarrel would get fed up with the guys in Augusta, Georgia, those were the words of encouragement her mother so often repeated. And just when Dorothy needed to break the monotony of going out with the local boys, her brother-in-law, Raworth, offered to set her up on a blind date with a friend who was coming to town on business. While there, the man planned to visit Raworth.

There's no doubt that Dorothy thought the world of her brother-in-law and would do anything for him. But accepting a blind date? Well, she had to think twice. For one, after asking repeatedly, "Tell me something about him. What does he look like, Raworth?" the only answer she got was, "Take my word for it, he's just a good ol' boy!"

Had Raworth been more specific, Dorothy might not have been so apprehensive. But under the circumstances, Dorothy had no idea what she might be getting herself into. After Raworth's constant begging, Dorothy decided, *By going, I have nothing to lose so I might as well say yes.* "Okay, Raworth, "I'll go under one condition, you and my sister will have to go with us."

"No problem! We'll be more than happy to," Raworth told her.

However, it wasn't until she agreed to accept the blind date that Raworth confessed, "Well, Dorothy, I have to tell you, he has one eye that kind of goes out to the right, sort of like a lazy eye, but it will be okay. In fact, you probably won't even notice it."

Oh, my word, Dorothy murmured, *This is the first and last time I'll get conned into something like this. This guy is going to be a real nerd. I just know it.* Already, she wanted this evening to be over. The sad fact was it had not even begun.

But when they all gathered and Dorothy Jarrel laid eyes on this man, her attitude quickly changed. Obviously, Raworth was only teasing Dorothy when he characterized his buddy as having an eye abnormality because Claude Estes turned out to be the best-looking man she had ever seen. To hear her describe him, "He was absolutely gorgeous. Tall, blond curly hair, and the prettiest blue eyes you ever saw. Why Claude resembled an Arrow Collar man. He could've posed in a neat and tidy button-down and advertised Arrow™ shirts on billboards nationwide!"

Miss Dorothy Jarrel also rated high in appearance. The brown-eyed, brunette stood 5'7" and was well within her average weight.

As the evening progressed, Raworth and Maudie wondered why they bothered tagging along. From observing their interaction, it didn't appear Claude and Dorothy needed chaperones. They talked and laughed all through dinner, practically ignoring their guests. The night Dorothy once dreaded evolved into an evening she hoped would never end. But because Claude lived out of town and would be leaving soon, Dorothy was careful not to build her expectations.

At evening's end when they were saying goodnight, she was delighted Claude asked, "Would you see me tomorrow night?"

Unfortunately, she had to decline. "I'm sorry. I already have plans tomorrow night."

Claude suggested, "Perhaps you could come home

early."

Dorothy thought about it for a moment and then agreed, "Well, maybe I can."

Normally, she wouldn't do this. But on occasion, Dorothy made exceptions. If she wanted to see another beau that same night, she would arrange to get home early. And as she put it, "Claude Estes was worth coming home for."

Since Dorothy planned two dates in one evening, she referred to her first escort as Bachelor No. 1, and labeled Claude Bachelor No. 2

After seeing a movie with Bachelor No. 1, Dorothy came up with a lame excuse to get home early. Wouldn't you know, just when Dorothy was standing on her front porch saying goodnight to Bachelor No. 1, Claude pulled into the driveway! At that point, the first young boy became curious.

"Who is that?" he asked

His question caught Dorothy off guard. Before she could even think, she'd said, "Oh, he's here to see my older sister Maudie."

What this young man didn't know was Maudie hadn't lived there in years. She resided with her husband, Raworth. Thank goodness the fellow never knew the difference.

As soon as Bachelor No. 1 drove out of sight, Dorothy Jarrel jumped in the car with Claude. For two hours they cruised Augusta, talking and learning more about each other. Claude was twenty-four and the oldest of four children. Birmingham, Alabama was home, yet he rarely spent time there. As a salesman for a national food company, he was required to travel much of the Southeast. While soul-searching and trying to decide which college to attend, Dorothy, the youngest in her family, worked full-time as a bank teller.

During their drive through Augusta, they covered

many different subjects. But one untouched topic puzzled Dorothy...Claude. He seemed interested, yet showed no affection, and he made no comments to indicate he held feelings for her.

The next day he left and mentioned nothing about ever seeing her again. Dorothy didn't know what to think. She thought they'd had a great time together.

Three weeks later, the entire scenario changed. While babysitting her niece and nephew, Dorothy received a surprise phone call. It was Claude. He said, "I called you at home and your mother told me I could reach you at Raworth's house. I'll be in Augusta next week, and I want a date every night."

By now, Dorothy had learned to court with caution. Under no circumstances would she inconvenience herself or anyone else for Claude who, in her opinion, was unpredictable. Before leaving town the last time, he made no future promises. Now three weeks had passed before she'd heard from him again. Besides, Dorothy didn't want to risk ruining her chances with the local boys for a fly-by-night fellow.

Without hesitation, she stated, "I'm just as sorry as I can be. I've got a date every night next week."

"Well", he told her, "Break them."

As tough as Dorothy tried to be, she wound up giving in. How could she say no to such a handsome man? After applying careful thought, she said, "I won't break them, but I'll give you a late date."

The next week when Claude arrived, he and Dorothy got together every night...of course, after she had returned home from her first date.

Then came Saturday, December 15th, 1938. The Forrest Hills Resort Hotel was hosting Augusta's annual Christmas Ball, and Dorothy had invited Claude. He looked spectacular in his new tuxedo, and Dorothy was a knock-out out in her silky black gown. A red flower decorated the waist, and the white corsage Claude brought and pinned to her upper left shoulder made her look lovelier.

Dressed to the nines, they got in the car and headed down Broad Street. As Claude made a right turn off Broad and started traveling over the Fifth Street Bridge, Dorothy exclaimed, "This isn't the way to the Forrest Hills Hotel."

"I realize that! But Aiken, South Carolina is this way, isn't it?"

Dorothy answered, "Yes. Aiken is this way. But what's in Aiken?"

Continuing down Fifth and crossing the Savannah River, Claude stated, "Well, I'm leaving for California tomorrow and I don't know when I'll get back. I'm just afraid you won't be available for me when I return. Why don't we go on over to South Carolina and get married? I don't have three days to wait for a marriage license in Georgia."

At last, true confessions. Though she'd kept quiet about her feelings, Dorothy fell in love with Claude the first second she saw him. Through Claude's suggestion of marriage, she assumed he must be crazy about her too; but his proposal baffled her so, she suffered a loss for words. As they rode in silence, Dorothy didn't answer yes or no.

Around ten forty-five p.m., they arrived in the sleepy town of Aiken, South Carolina. Of course City Hall was closed, but they found a gas station still open. They went in and asked the clerk if he knew where a Justice of the Peace lived. The gentleman nodded, then gave them directions. By the time they reached the man's home, it was midnight; but that didn't stop them from knocking on His Honor's door.

A few minutes later, the door slowly opened; and there stood a short man, wearing bedroom slippers and an old-fashioned bath robe that resembled an Indian blanket. Wearily, he answered, "Yes?"

Dorothy let Claude do the talking. He told the Justice of the Peace that he and Dorothy wanted to get married right away. After Claude explained his situation and the fact that they didn't have three days to wait for a marriage license in Georgia, the Magistrate looked sternly at them and said, "I don't make it my practice to get out of bed and issue a marriage license at midnight; but in your case, I'll go ahead and do it."

He invited Claude and Dorothy into his home. To add some spark to their midnight rendezvous, the man threw another a log onto the dwindling flame in the fireplace, then plugged in the Christmas tree lights. Childrens' stockings and mistletoe hung from the mantle. Standing in front of the hearth, the Justice of the Peace performed the ceremony.

In no time at all, Dorothy and Claude had exchanged vows, been pronounced husband and wife, and issued their official marriage license. For this couple to wed, *Good Looks Was All It Took*. Before leaving, Dorothy made a wisecrack that had them all chuckling. "Had I had the slightest inkling I'd be getting married tonight, I would've worn a white gown instead of this slinky black dress!"

On the trip home, things weren't so funny. Awakening to the reality of what she'd just done, Dorothy's humor faded and she fell silent. The more miles they traveled, the more she thought. *Is Claude Estes capable of supporting us? And on the morrow, I'll be leaving for California. Am I prepared to say good-bye to my family and friends?* Until now, she had been in a dream world.

By the time they reached Augusta, it was two o'clock in the morning. Their first stop was Dorothy's home. When the newlyweds walked in, Dorothy's mother was awake and in the den talking to her Aunt Nellie. Mrs.

Jarrel asked, "Well, how was the dance?"

Dorothy, still in a state of shock, announced, "Well, we didn't quite get there, and we have something to tell you. We've just been to Aiken and we got married!"

"You're kidding me," Mrs. Jarrel shouted, her mouth hanging wide open.

Dorothy assured her, "No, Momma. It's true. Here's the marriage license to prove it."

Mrs. Jarrel had to see it to believe it. After glancing at the license, she turned to Claude and said, "She's my baby."

Claude quickly claimed possession. "Well, she's my baby now."

"Well, you take good care of her."

"Don't you worry," Claude assured Mrs. Jarrel, "she's in the best of hands."

While Claude stayed in the den and talked to Mrs. Jarrel, Aunt Nellie followed Dorothy into her bedroom. Claude was registered at the Richmond Hotel, so Aunt Nellie helped Dorothy pack. As soon as they were out of earshot, Dorothy fell apart. "Oh, Aunt Nellie, I'm so nervous. I don't know what I've done! All I know is I think he's wonderful and I'm crazy about him."

When it came to successful marriages, Aunt Nellie had forty years invested. She sat on the side of Dorothy's bed, grabbed her hand and said, "Well, if you're crazy about him, then everything will be all right."

That comforting statement was the exact reason everyone loved Aunt Nellie. She was wonderful with words, and had always served as Dorothy's guidepost. What she told her niece that night had a lasting effect. Before eloping, Claude and Dorothy only knew each other two weeks, but during their fifty years of marriage, they raised four sons and a daughter.

Dorothy Jarrel Estes reminisced, "Yes, I'll never forget my mother's encouraging words," 'Dorothy, some day your knight is going to come riding through on a white horse and sweep you right off of your feet.'

"Well," she said, "Momma was right. My knight came through and swept me right off my feet, but he wasn't riding a white horse. Claude was driving a rental car."

INTRODUCTION TO STRANGER THAN FICTION

I had done my share of complaining about my tough times in Alabama, but had I never moved there, my chances for collecting the next chapter were nil.

The eve before I left St. Petersburg to relocate to Birmingham, my friends took me to dinner. And one of them, Karen, was all too familiar with my plans to write a book. The local newspaper had printed several love stories in a special Valentine's Day edition, and she brought a copy for me to keep. Because we were in a hurry to beat the crowd, I stuffed the paper in a duffel bag and forgot about it.

Around September, while staring out my living room window and admiring the autumn leaves as they fell onto the ground, I thought about the stories I had gathered and wondered where I might possibly collect a few more. Suddenly, it dawned on me that I still had the newspaper Karen had given me the night before I left St. Pete.

I jumped from my chair, ran into my bedroom and tore my closet apart digging for the duffel bag. After finding it underneath a stack of blankets, I pulled the paper out, read through it, and discovered a story that stood out among the rest. Below that particular article was a picture of the couple, including their names and the city where they resided.

Quickly, I dialed directory assistance. After spelling the couples' last name, I was not only confident I would collect this story, but absolutely astounded when the telephone operator commented, "Girl, that number popped right up. You know you're supposed to call these people."

STRANGER THAN FICTION

AT THE AGE OF FOURTEEN, life was a blast for Margaret Marshall and her best friend Betty. On a Friday night, in the summer of 1944, these silly schoolgirls were doing the Jitterbug in the living room of Margaret's home. The curtains were open, and anybody passing the house could see their grand performance.

All the while, Margaret and Betty were oblivious to the world around them when suddenly, applause, hollering and wolf whistling interrupted their good time. The girls had attracted a small audience. Three young boys, walking through the neighborhood, had stopped to admire the show.

For a minute, Margaret and Betty were red with embarrassment; but after the three onlookers motioned for them to come outside, the two entertainers didn't hesitate, and snickered all the way out the door.

Gathered in a huddle in Margaret's front yard, the teen-agers introduced themselves, all except for Don Kysor. He was the timid one who stood under the light pole. On the other hand, Frank Johnston, the leader of their pack, said they lived in the area. Oddly enough, Margaret and Betty had never seen them around. Other than discovering everyone shared the same neighborhood, the boys didn't give the girls a chance to learn much more about them because the extrovert, Frank Johnston, was just being a typical male when he asked the girls, "Well, which one of us do you like?"

While Betty kept quiet, Margaret minced no words and pointed to the young man in the distance. Diplomatically, she stated, "I like the one over there by the light pole."

For whatever reason, Margaret picked, Don, the shy guy. Because he had hardly spoken two words to them, Betty asked, "Hey, Margaret, what do you find so interesting about that guy?"

Margaret shrugged her shoulders and said, "I don't know. I just think he's cute."

At first, Don stayed to himself. But when his buddies pressed the issue by hollering, "Hey, Don, this one likes you," that was all the confidence this bashful boy needed. He quickly came out of seclusion and joined in the fun.

Within minutes, their group of five gradually diminished to a party of three. Betty frolicked with Frank and Martin while Don and Margaret drifted into their own little corner of the world. In the short time they talked, it became obvious that Don Kysor was not only smart, but also a hard worker. He wasn't old enough to drive a car, but that didn't stop him from sacking groceries part-time at the supermarket.

Watching his father struggle to support them through the Great Depression, Don Kysor learned to pinch pennies; and when he did spend his hard-earned money, it was usually in the form of a wise investment. With the extra cash he made working at the supermarket, Don bought war bonds. Along with that purchase, he received free movie tickets. The only thing he needed now was a date. And since Miss Margaret Marshall had boosted Don's ego by choosing him as her favorite fellow, she was the lucky lady that got invited to the theater.

After about a forty-five minute chat, it started getting late; and to avoid trouble, the boys needed to make their ten o'clock curfew, but not Don Kysor. He was more worried about getting Margaret's phone number than he was concerned about a stupid curfew. This once shy boy didn't budge until he wrote it down and tucked it in his shirt pocket. "I'll call you soon," he promised as he ran down the street to catch up with Frank and Martin.

Wearing an ear to ear smile, Margaret sauntered back into the house, her sidekick, Betty, trailing behind her. The smell of pork and homemade barbecue sauce led them into the kitchen where, Ina Marshall, Margaret's mom, was preparing for the next day's Fourth of July picnic. While Mrs. Marshall stirred the sauce, the girls sat at the kitchen table, eating cookies and laughing as they explained how the Jitterbug had won them an audience.

So filled with excitement, Margaret almost choked trying to swallow and talk at the same time. "Mother, I just met the cutest boy. His name is Don. I gave him our number because we're going to the movie together, so if I'm not here when he calls, please make sure you tell him what time I'll be home!"

If Margaret had agreed to go out with a guy she hardly knew, her description of Don as being "the cutest boy" just wasn't sufficient information to satisfy her mom. Ina Marshall demanded to know more. "How old is he?" she asked.

"The same age as me, mom—fourteen."

"And where does he live, Margaret?"

"Well, he used to live on Main Street; but about a year ago, he said his family moved over here to Hyde Park."

Before allowing her daughter permission, Ina Marshall directed one last question. "Do you mind telling me his last name?"

Margaret answered, "Kysor—His name is Don Kysor."

After hearing that, Ina Marshall pursed her lips to one side and raised her right brow. Something about the name "Kysor" seemed to ring a bell.

Margaret noticed the bizarre look on her mother's face and asked, "What is it, mom?"

"Did you say Kysor?"

"Yes, ma'am! What's the big deal?"

Smiling, but keeping her reasons secret, Ina Marshall told her daughter, "Before you go out with him, I would like to speak with his mother."

By now, Margaret was itching to know why her mother wanted to talk to Mrs. Kysor. To try and find out, she bribed her every way she knew how; but until Ina Marshall had a chance to speak with Don's mother, she wouldn't reveal one word.

The Fourth of July couldn't come fast enough, and Don called just as he had promised. After he and Margaret talked a few minutes and planned their movie date, she told him she didn't understand why, but her mother wished to speak with his. Immediately afterwards, Margaret handed the phone to her mom.

Evidently, Mrs. Marshall wanted to keep this conversation private because she took the telephone, pulled the cord as far as it would stretch, stepped out of the kitchen and into their laundry room, and motioned for Margaret to leave. Of course, Margaret pretended to exit the room; but as soon as her mother shut the laundry room door, she quietly crept back into the kitchen. With her head pressed to the wall, Margaret strained to listen. She gathered bits and pieces of the conversation, but not enough to make sense out of any of it.

While eavesdropping, she overheard her mother laugh and say, "Yeah, I remember she wouldn't eat, and we could never get him to stop. This is really a surprise. I can't believe it!"

With all the cackling, Margaret said it sounded as though their mothers were celebrating some sort of reunion. They rambled on for fifteen minutes, then Margaret could tell they were about to end their conversation when she heard her mom say, "Don't wait this long. Let's stay in touch, Ruby."

So Mrs. Marshall wouldn't catch Margaret standing

outside the door listening, she fled the kitchen and fooled her mom into thinking she'd been in her bedroom all that time. After hanging up the phone, Ina Marshall yelled down the hall, "Margaret, come here. You're never going to believe this!"

As Margaret strolled back into the kitchen and sat down at the table, her mother unveiled the shocking truth. Don Kysor and Margaret Marshall had an encounter long before that hot summer night in July of 1944. However, at their first sight of contact, both were too young to even realize the world was turning.

On a bitter cold day in New York, January 28th, 1929, Ruby Kysor gave birth to her son Don. Just three days later, January 31st, Ina Marshall delivered a healthy seven pound baby girl and named her Margaret. While Don Kysor and Margaret Marshall lay side by side in the nursery at Niagara Falls Memorial Hospital, their mothers shared a semi-private room down the hall.

Now, the bits and pieces of the conversation Margaret gathered between her mother and Mrs. Kysor made sense. When Mrs. Marshall made the comment, "Yeah, I remember she wouldn't eat, and we could never get him to stop," she was talking about when the nurses brought their babies in to be fed.

Amazing! This was by far the most astonishing news Margaret had ever learned. Obviously, it was much more than Don's good looks that caught Margaret's attention. Like a magnet clings to metal, fate drew Margaret Marshall to the shy boy standing under the light pole.

With permission from both parents and free tickets, Don and Margaret saw a movie, and that Friday evening marked their first official date. From that night and for the next six years, they became inseparable steadies.

As he lay in an incubator in the hospital's nursery shortly after his birth on January 28th, 1929, Don Kysor was too infantile to understand his little bride-to-be would soon arrive. But twenty years later and just a few months before their wedding, an event of September 23rd, 1950, he wrote Margaret Marshall the following:

Little did our mothers know when we were born that day,
that we were to be united and never torn away.
Pretty soon the day will come when we will say "I do."
That's when you'll belong to me and I'll belong to you.
I'm waiting dear, impatiently for that great day to come,
For we'll never be parted after the ceremony is done.
From that day on till when we die, I'll be the happiest
man alive.
For I'll have you and you'll have me, and to keep it
that way I'll strive.

Don Kysor was a man of his word. When he wrote that poem in 1950, he held true to his promise.

Who would have ever thought two babies, born three days apart in the same hospital, their mothers sharing a semi-private room down the hall, would meet fourteen years later in their neighborhood, fall madly in love and eventually marry? Sometimes facts *are* stranger than fiction!

MAKING CENTS OUT OF NONSENSE

Since I'd borrowed enough money to survive June, July, and August, I spent the entire summer posting fliers in bridal shops, calling churches, and beating the streets to collect unusual marriage stories. By mid-September, I knew it was time to get a job and start repaying the loan. Paranoid from the rotten luck I'd had with court reporting, I decided to try my hand at something different so I contacted a personnel agency and told the woman I spoke with that I was only interested in temporary work because I did hope to find employment in the field which I was trained.

After briefing her on my educational background, the woman asked me if I would accept a permanent position with a company if the pay was decent. I didn't really want to quit court reporting, but thinking about all I had been through trying to make a living at it, I told her, "If someone offered me a job with a salary I could survive on, I would definitely consider taking it."

She told me she had to set up some interviews and that she would be in touch soon. Around noon the next day, the lady called and gave me the name of the place where I was to interview. She named the company, gave their address and told me what time to be there, and I was planning on going...until she announced the name of the person who would be conducting the interview. *Oh, no! This would never work. Someone from my past — to whom I did not have the best relationship — was the absolute last person I wanted or needed to go to and ask for a job.*

Of course, I wasn't about to let the woman from the

personnel agency in on my secret, so I played along with her plan by saying, "Thank you. I'll be there." But I immediately began praying that God would get me out of it.

No more than fifteen minutes later, a kind lady, who I'd spoken with months earlier about court reporting – and who had absolutely nothing available at the time – called and offered me work. With a truly legitimate reason, I called the personnel agency and canceled that dreaded interview that I would have somehow wiggled out of anyway.

So here I was Making Cents Out Of Nonsense. Of all the places I could work while writing a book on happy marriages, I landed a job in divorce court. And the only person I could possibly solicit a story from there was a circuit court judge.

BOUND BY DESTINY

THE YEAR WAS 1970. THE Brady Bunch was among America's most watched sitcoms. The Osmond Brothers were on a record setting roll. Hot pants, bell bottom jeans, and baggy velour shirts were en vogue.

Lorie Lyle's Alma Mater, John Carroll High School, was celebrating their homecoming football game. To keep warm through a nippy November night, she stopped at the mall on her way home from school to purchase a velour shirt. Originally made for boys, but popular among both genders, the soft, comfortable sportswear was only sold in the men's department. So when Lorie entered the store, she headed straight into men's clothing.

There, hanging on the rack, were a number of velours in a variety of different colors. After browsing, she picked out a couple and walked towards the dressing room. Lorie was moving right along and minding her own business when suddenly, in a loud voice, the store clerk hollered, "Just what do you think you're doing? You can't go in there. That's the men's dressing room."

The clerk's loud and demeaning tone of voice startled Lorie; but instead of becoming frightened or embarrassed, she felt her modesty had been insulted, and she got mad. Sarcastically, Lorie spouted off, "Good grief! What's your problem? I'm not disrobing. I'm simply trying these shirts on *over* my clothes."

After discovering this feisty customer took no verbal punches, the store clerk backed down. "Okay! If all you're doing is trying them on *over* your clothes, go right ahead."

Of course, once she'd tried the shirts on, decided to buy them, and walked to the register to pay, the young man had changed his attitude. In a cordial tone, he commented, "You know, you look very familiar."

"Yeah," Lorie told him, "so do you." The sales clerk, who later introduced himself as Alton DeJames, knew he'd never seen Lorie before. Because she not only had a fabulous figure, but was tall, had long blond hair, and brown eyes that practically spoke with expression, Alton was only doing what any other sensible man would do around an unusually attractive lady—trying to make conversation. However, when Lorie told the clerk he had a familiar face also, she wasn't blowing smoke. Since the store clerk had played linebacker for Auburn University, Lorie had recognized his picture in the newspapers. Judging from a black and white photograph, he looked good; but in person, Alton DeJames was awesome. Tall, brown hair, brown eyes, and the body of a linebacker, Lorie, like most other women, would give her last breath for just one date with the handsome athlete.

While Alton sacked the velour shirts, he started quizzing Lorie.

"Where do you go to high school?" he asked.

"Well, I graduated from John Carroll last year. But tonight is their homecoming, and I'm going to the game."

Because it happened to be mid-afternoon, business was slack; and Alton had no one else to wait on so he continued making small talk with his foxy female customer. Out of all the questions Alton asked, Lorie hoped one would at least be for her phone number. Since he didn't, and she had to hurry home and get ready for the football game, she used her smarts by casually mentioning that her father owned a barbecue restaurant down the street. That way if Alton wanted to get in touch, he knew where to find her.

Unfortunately, he never once hinted for Lorie's phone number, nor did he inquire as to whether she had a boyfriend. With no reason whatsoever to bank on seeing or even hearing from Alton DeJames, Lorie left the department store believing that she would soon be dating him. As far as an explanation to back her thoughts...well, only time would tell.

Having such a confident air about it, she busted through the front door of her home and shouted to her sister, who happened to be sitting in the family room watching television, "Hey, Carol, guess what? I just met Alton DeJames and I have a strong feeling that before long, we're going to go out."

Of course, anybody who followed Auburn football in the late Sixties and early Seventies had heard of the Tiger's outstanding linebacker, so it wasn't necessary for Lorie to elaborate or go into great detail to describe how incredibly good-looking Alton DeJames happened to be. And though Lorie Lyle had an instinct they would go out soon, she had no inkling as to how, when, or where they might meet. After all, she certainly couldn't initiate contact. Her parents were from the old school and had reared their daughters to understand that, around their house, calling boys was a *no-no*. Her only hope was that he might drop by her father's barbecue restaurant while she was there.

Unfortunately, a couple of weeks passed and Lorie had neither seen nor heard from Alton. But shortly thereafter, fate took a unique turn and caught Lorie Lyle by total surprise. One day, while working in the jewelry department at a large retail store, Lorie came to know another employee, Fran, who'd been hired as an extra through the Christmas holidays. In between customers, they chatted.

"Are you in school?" Lorie asked.

"Yeah," said Fran. "I'm a sophomore at Auburn."

"Do you date anybody?"

Fran answered, "Yeah. I've been going out with Alton DeJames."

"Oh, really!" Lorie exclaimed. "I met him a couple of weeks ago. He seems like a real nice guy."

But under that facade Lorie thought, *What a rare coincidence. Out of all the students enrolled at Auburn University, it would be my luck to work with the girl who's dating the man of my dreams.* However, that coincidence was nowhere near as bizarre as the next. Seconds later, while speaking of the Auburn linebacker, Lorie glanced towards the store's entrance and saw Alton DeJames walking through the door! At first he didn't recognize Lorie; but once he got directly in front of the jewelry counter and saw her standing behind it, he looked baffled and even shouted, "I didn't know you worked here."

Right about the time Alton stopped to talk to Lorie, Fran walked over and included herself in their conversation. What an awkward situation. For the next few minutes, they all three stood and talked, and it appeared Alton would rather flirt with Lorie than, Fran, the girl he *supposedly* dated.

Fortunately for Lorie, another customer approached and Fran excused herself to wait on them. Just when Lorie thought she'd gotten a lucky break and could talk to Alton without interruption, a slap across the shoulder diverted his attention. Two of his fraternity brothers, who happened to be passing through the store, recognized Alton and stopped to say hello. Of course he stepped away from the counter and spoke with his college clones.

By this time, Lorie felt all odds were against her ever going out with Alton DeJames. After all, for the past two weeks, she'd been hoping he would walk into her father's restaurant while she was there. When that didn't pan out, she entertained the thought of returning to the department store where they initially met and purchasing a few more velours, but she didn't want to appear desperate. Out of all the ideas Lorie concocted, she never once imagined Alton would walk into her workplace.

Since everyone else was preoccupied and it was almost closing time, Lorie began balancing her register. As she counted the change in her cash drawer, the manager announced over the intercom that the store would soon be closing. Out of the corner of her eye, Lorie could see Alton waving good-bye to his fraternity brothers. And before she could shut her register drawer, he recoursed to the jewelry counter. Fran, who was part-time help and not a salaried employee, had gone to the office to clock out. Before she had time to return, Alton leaned across the counter and asked, "Lorie, would you like to go out?"

At this point, Lorie Lyle had become totally confused. Under the assumption that Alton dated Fran, not to mention the fact he'd spent the last ten minutes talking with two of his fraternity brothers, Lorie naturally assumed Alton wanted to set her up with one of his buddies. Unsure, she asked, "With who?"

"Who do you think? With me!" he answered.

Ecstatic over the fact Alton had finally invited her out, but at the same time a little frazzled about the *other woman*, Lorie questioned him, "Aren't you dating Fran?"

"Not anymore. We used to date, but now we're just friends. She doesn't have a car so I stopped by to give her a ride home tonight. That's the only reason I'm here," Alton assured her.

Lorie breathed a sigh of relief. Certainly, after the worry and hassle of trying to track this man down, Lorie Lyle wasn't about to refuse his invitation. Of course, after she graciously accepted, Alton confessed to Lorie that he'd been looking for her. "You know, I stopped by your father's restaurant a couple of times hoping to find you there. Go ahead and give me your number so I don't have to go through that again."

What sneaks! Before Fran returned, Lorie had jotted her number down on the back of a price tag, and Alton stuck it in his wallet. If only Fran had known.

Emotions were hot between Alton and Lorie just before Christmas, 1970, when they celebrated their first date, but passions ran even hotter during their two year courtship. With both having outstanding qualities that complimented the other, the fact that Alton was a devout Catholic impressed Lorie the most because throughout her teens, most of the guys she'd dated were Protestants, not that she had anything against that. However, since Lorie was Catholic also, she had hoped to marry within her religion. Her wish came true the moment Alton proposed.

Brought together by fate and *Bound by Destiny*, unusual encounters that seemed to connect this couple were far from over. After becoming engaged, an event of utmost significance occurred that shocked, not only Alton and Lorie, but the entire DeJames family. Following dinner one Friday evening, Alton and Lorie decided, on a whim, to stop by his parents house.

It just so happened that his mother and father had dragged out their old projector and were up watching family films from years past, and nothing thrilled Lorie more than to see slides of Alton as a small boy. But when they came across the picture of Alton's sister, Debbie, at her First Communion, something in the film struck them as being strange. There stood Debbie, her religious education teacher, and Debbie's best friend, but they had difficulty identifying the little girl in the slide who had stepped in front of the camera to wave. In an attempt to figure out who this child was, Mr. DeJames kept the projector focused on that particular slide while everyone carefully studied it.

"She certainly has some big, brown eyes," Mrs. DeJames blurted.

Big, brown eyes "Wait! Hold it right there," said Alton.

Obviously, Mrs. DeJames's comment was the clue that helped solve the mystery. It was hard for this child to hide behind her most outstanding feature. Those big, gorgeous brown eyes were recognized by none other than the man who'd, so often, lovingly gazed into them. "Lorie, that's you!" Alton shouted.

Sure enough, there stood Lorie Lyle wearing the long white dress her parents bought for her First Communion. A mere eight year old at that time, and not a child of spontaneity, Lorie Lyle had absolutely no idea when she included herself in a picture approximately twelve years earlier, that she was standing beside her sister-in-law-to-be and waving to her future father-in-law.

A romance that once had minor difficulty catching fire and leaving ground, eventually ignited and shot off like a fireworks display. Not only did sparks fly between this couple at the department store where they initially met, sparks literally flew between Alton and Lorie DeJames on January 8th, 1972 when they cut into their wedding cake and Lorie's veil fell into one of the burning candles and caught on fire.

Of course, Alton, who'd no sooner than an hour earlier promised to honor Lorie in sickness and in health, came to the rescue and extinguished the flame. But the other blaze that ignited, he's been careful not to destroy. Through the past forty plus years of marriage and the rearing of three children, Alton DeJames *has kept* the home fires burning.

LOVE AT FIRST SIGHT

T HE YEAR WAS 1931, AND Erich Saüer, a civil engineer, was thirty-two years of age. The history buff, who wanted to see the world was granted his opportunity when the industrial company that employed Erich eventually promoted him, and the new position required him to leave his German roots and start anew in Argentina.

On the day he was to depart, and hours before his ship set sail, Erich made rounds to visit close relatives and bid a final farewell. And as he was leaving his cousin Bernard's home, his attention was drawn to a photograph that had been placed on the coffee table. After picking the frame up, holding it gently in his hand while gazing at the young, blue-eyed blond, Erich gasped, "Ahhh! Who is that? I love her!"

"That's Elsbeth Grunewald. We're related by marriage," said Bernard.

"I want to meet her."

"She lives just down the street. Come on," Bernard offered, "I'll take you there."

In no time at all, Bernard and Erich were knocking on the Grünewalds door. Once Elsbeth answered, as far as Erich was concerned, Argentina didn't seem so exciting after all. As he eloquently put it, "Her body was as beautiful as her face in the photograph."

Being the polite eighteen year old that she was, Elsbeth cordially invited Bernard and Erich inside, then she and her mother served them coffee and cake. During their two hour visit, it never dawned on Elsbeth that Bernard's purpose for stopping over was solely for Erich

Saüer's benefit, yet it was Erich, himself, that dropped an obvious hint of interest when, just before leaving, he walked over to Elsbeth, grabbed her hand, kissed it, then said, "I'm going to marry you some day."

Once she had shut the door behind him, Elsbeth stood in exasperation and even shouted to her mother, who was standing no more than six feet away from her, "Mom, did you see what just happened? That guy is crazy! How's a man, who doesn't even know me and is leaving for another country, think he's going to marry me? Besides, I'm eighteen. He's thirty-two. With that much of an age difference, it would never work."

In the short time Elsbeth got to spend with Erich, she only saw him with her physical eyes and did not get the chance to know him intimately. However, in the couple of months that followed, Elsbeth saw Erich in a completely different light when the letters he had written to her began pouring in on almost a daily basis. Suddenly, age and distance made no difference. After discovering his heart and soul through written correspondence, Elsbeth fell in love.

Then, about ten months after they'd met, Elsbeth received a small package from Erich. Inside she discovered an engagement ring, a written proposal of marriage, along with a ticket to Argentina. Those numerous, irresistible love letters Elsbeth had received from Erich was enough to convince her there was no man on earth she'd rather be with. In late September, 1932, and with her parents consent, Elsbeth said good-bye to family and close friends, boarded a ship, then left her country to sail halfway around the world to join the man she'd once called *crazy!*

While traveling the rough seas those few weeks, Elsbeth, full of anticipation, could only imagine how wonderful it was going to be when she would finally meet and greet Erich upon her arrival to Argentina.

However, excitement turned into sheer disbelief and disappointment when her ship finally sailed into port.

Around that time, many male adults were snatching young women as they arrived in the city, then taking them off and raping them. To crack down on crime, officials at Immigration could not release underage females unless they had the proper paperwork, were claimed by an adult, or showed proof that they were married.

Unfortunately, when Elsbeth disembarked, authorities met her at the gate. After intense questioning, they informed Elsbeth her paperwork had been filled out incorrectly and did not comply with their rules and regulations, which left her with two choices: Return to Germany, or get married. After traveling for weeks just to get there, Elsbeth wasn't about to return to Europe, certainly not without Erich. And of course they planned to eventually marry, but it was never their intention to be forced or coerced.

While Elsbeth, alone and frightened, was being held overnight by the officials at Immigration, Erich was outside the gate pleading with authorities to release her into his custody. "I'll marry her right now!" Erich shouted.

One of the officers asked, "Where are you going to find a preacher at this late hour?"

Terrified Elsbeth would return to Germany, Erich was unable to think rationally. But once he realized what the officer had said, Erich wondered, *Where will I find a preacher at this hour? It's almost midnight.* With his head hung low, and wearing the longest face, Erich went home. But just before sunrise the next morning, he returned to the Immigration department, accompanied by a Justice of the Peace.

Once authorities released her, Elsbeth felt as though she'd been freed from captivity and clutched Erich as though she truly had been. The Justice of the Peace performed a short ceremony, but Elsbeth and Erich, having both been raised Presbyterians, did not feel legally wed unless they were formally married before a preacher inside a church. After searching, they found the Protestant church in a predominantly Catholic community and made an appointment to get married in the style which they preferred.

On the day they were to wed, Erich and Elsbeth, along with two witnesses, were sitting on the front pew inside the church, waiting patiently for the preacher. Once the minister entered the sanctuary, Erich immediately jumped up, ran over to him, threw his arm around the man, and both of them talked, laughed and joked as though they were long, lost friends. As it turned out, Erich and the minister *were* long, lost friends. They'd known each other as small boys, but had lost contact through the years. Amazing! The kid Erich once wrestled with growing up, was about to pronounce he and Elsbeth man and wife.

Of all dates to choose to get married, Elsbeth and Erich selected the day everyone else in the world shys away from—Friday, October 13th, 1932. Venturing from the norm with a completely different outlook, Erich and Elsbeth both agreed: "We're going to start with luck and love and refuse to let tradition's superstition interfere."

Determined to beat the odds, Erich and Elsbeth conquered all because not only did they bring five smart, lovely and talented children into the world during their fifty years of marriage, their long and blissful life together was free of unwonted interruption.

Unfortunately, all good things must end. Shortly after celebrating their Golden Wedding Anniversary in 1982, Erich fell ill and passed away. Though Elsbeth yearned for Erich, there was something valuable and irreplaceable that kept him alive. On display in the living room of her home was the picture Erich fell in love with in

1931. Elsbeth would pick it up off the table, stare into it, shake her head in amazement and say, "It's hard to imagine...before marrying, I only spent two hours with Erich. And to think, fifty years of fond memories and it all began with my photograph."

INTRODUCTION TO
THE BEST KEPT SECRET

Having lived in Florida for a period of time, I became a big Florida State football fan. I'd heard Bobby and Ann Bowden had an unusual marriage story, and I'd fantasized about collecting it. But, realistically, I had a life-size picture of me calling the athletic department at Florida State and envisioning Bobby Bowden running off the field from practice to grab the telephone and explain to me how he met his wife, Ann.

But when I walked into a fast-food restaurant on March 2nd, 1996, I witnessed an event that, to this day, has left me flabbergasted. I used to rarely ever eat breakfast, but that morning just happened to be one of the days that I did. After placing my order at the register, I moved to the left of the counter so the fellow behind me could place his and couldn't help but notice that the man was wearing a garnet colored wind breaker. The gold emblem on the upper left pocket of the jacket featured the school's mascot, Chief Osceola, sitting high atop the horse they call Renegade. I turned to him and said, "I sure do like your jacket, and I love the Florida State Seminoles!"

"Yeah," he responded. "Bobby Bowden and I go way back. We grew up together and have remained very good friends throughout the years."

To me, that was enough of a shock. But when he pulled out his wallet and showed me a picture of himself with Bobby Bowden and a few other friends on a Panama City Beach in 1949, I worried they'd have to wire my jaw shut.

While I had the opportunity, I formally introduced myself, briefly mentioned *Marriages Meant To Be* and asked the gentleman if he might could help me obtain their story for the book. He held out his arm, shook my hand, said his name was Roy Vance, and that he'd be delighted to help. He also informed me that Bobby and Ann were extremely hard to reach, but if I'd give him a week or two, he'd have an answer.

As fate would have it, on March 2nd, 1996, while waiting in line for breakfast inside a mobbed fast-food restaurant, I got more than a ham biscuit. I collected my last chapter.

THE BEST KEPT SECRET

DURING THE 1940'S WHEN THE steel industry was booming, George Estock accepted a job that would move him from Gadsden, a small town in northeast Alabama, to the city lights of Birmingham. Having to transfer his daughter, Ann, to a different high school in her sophomore year was something he hated doing; but supporting the family took priority. Besides, George Estock didn't need to worry because Ann never met a stranger; and judging from the vast number of friends she had, he knew she would easily adjust elsewhere. With her father's dark hair and hazel green eyes, combined with her mother's good looks and sense of humor, Ann was not only beautiful, she bubbled with personality.

As her father assumed, after they moved to Birmingham and enrolled Ann in school, the new kid on the block fit in just fine. By the time football season rolled around, Ann Estock's new friends had taught her every chant and cheer and welcomed her to the Woodlawn High School cheerleading squad. Yet school wasn't the only place where Ann made friends. Around their house, Sunday was a day of worship; and the first thing the Estocks did after relocating was join Ruhama Baptist Church. Through her active involvement with the choir and youth group, Ann widened her social circle, which included a multitude of suitors.

So when Ruhama Baptist Church sponsored their annual wiener roast, Ann had no problem finding an escort. Though Ann chose to go with a boy named Ben, she was admired that evening by many other fellows, one in particular being Bobby Bowden. To this day, Bobby can recall the green and white striped jump suit Ann was wearing that Friday evening fifty years ago, yet Ann Estock was no stranger to him. With Bobby playing half-back for the Woodlawn High School football team and Ann a member of the cheerleading squad, he had certainly spotted her on the field and in the halls. Even while sitting on the back row with his buddies during church on Sundays, Bobby observed Ann singing from the choir loft. Since he lived just down the street from her, occasionally he, along with a neighbor friend, would stand under the street light beside Ann's house and pitch rocks onto her front porch to catch her attention.

Though Bobby had had his eyes on Ann for a while, he hadn't quite formulated a plan on how to confidently approach the beautiful and bubbly sophomore. Furthermore, being Ann was only fourteen, Bobby was unsure as to whether she had her parents consent to date or if she was restricted to just meeting boys at church and school functions. But one thing was for certain: After seeing her with Ben at the church wiener roast and then mulling over what to do, Bobby Bowden decided that it wouldn't be long before ol' Ben would soon be *been gone*.

Lucky for him, a few months later, when Bobby learned Ann had turned fifteen and had her father's permission to date on a limited basis, he was first in line to ask her out. For the next two years, without any glitches, Ann and Bobby dated steady, rarely missing church on Sunday, the prom, and numerous Friday night movies at the Alabama Theater, never skipping a trip afterwards to the popular Polar Bear for their favorite ice cream swirls. Even after Bobby graduated from high school and left for the University of Alabama, he cut classes on Friday afternoons and returned to Birmingham to see his girl. Like destined soul mates, it was basically a given around the community that Ann and Bobby would one day marry.

However, trouble in paradise began shortly after Bobby and a few buddies spent spring break together. For extra cash during their week off from college, a farmer in a small Alabama town paid Bobby and his friends to hoe corn. Wringing wet with sweat from the afternoon heat, Bobby and the rest of the boys stripped down to their underwear. When the farmer stepped outside and caught them almost nude, he got hot enough to fire them. Instead of packing up and heading home, this little group of daredevils hitchhiked to Panama City Beach, Florida and partied the remainder of the week.

While Ann stayed in Birmingham and spent her spring break working as a sales person in the record department at the five and dime store, she felt certain Bobby was slaving on an Alabama farm. However, she was in for a rude awakening the following week when a male acquaintance dropped by her workplace to chat and informed Ann that he and some friends had just returned from Panama City, and briefly mentioned meeting a few fellows from Woodlawn while on their beach jaunt. As he continued talking, the boy boasted and bragged about all the girls they met and what a good time they'd had on their trip, then he made a grave mistake by naming the guys in attendance. Knowing Ann attended Woodlawn, but unaware of the fact that she and Bobby were sweethearts, the fellow happened to rattle off the Bowden name, and Ann could feel a war waging on the home front.

"Beg your pardon? Did you say Bobby Bowden?" Ann asked.

"Sure did."

Why that rascal! she thought. All the time Ann assumed Bobby was hoeing corn, he had actually been flirting with and watching other girls on a Panama City Beach.

Oh, mercy! Bobby's excursion to Florida was going to cost him.

Although she was raging mad, Ann just let the boy ramble, and never once admitted that she and Bobby dated steady. But as soon as he left the five and dime store, she telephoned Bobby and instructed him to pick her up. After making him treat her to a meal and a movie, Ann then proceeded to give Bobby a piece of her mind and chastised him for cheating on her.

Bobby explained that since he was away at college, he wished to date other people. That suited Ann fine. If Bobby was going to be unfaithful, they might as well break up. Besides, Ann Estock was an independent female, full of pride, and the last thing she wanted Bobby Bowden to think was that a parting of the ways would bother her. Before the night was over, they mutually agreed to date other people.

But in the few weeks that followed, Bobby began having second thoughts about breaking up with Ann, especially when he attended Woodlawn High School's spring fashion show and all the other boys in the auditorium screamed and whistled when Ann modeled down the runway in a royal blue gaberdine suit. While Ann pivoted left, then right, Irving Berlin's hit tune *A Pretty Girl Is Like A Melody,* played in the background, and Bobby's heart sank.

However, the real kicker was the weekend Bobby returned from college and invited another girl to go on a date. Parked a few cars down from them that Friday evening at the drive-in movie sat Ann and her new beau. So gut-wrenched over seeing Ann with another fellow, Bobby practically ignored his date and constantly stared down into the car where Ann was sitting, carefully watching her every move. Worse than the horror movie on the screen was the horror thought Bobby had of his former girlfriend possibly becoming seriously involved with someone else. Unable to stand the sight or thought of Ann with another, Bobby asked himself, *What have I done?*

Not the kind to accept defeat, and an absolute natural for picking a winner, Bobby Bowden suddenly realized he'd had a prize in Ann Estock and was a fool to ever let her go. Like the adrenaline rush of trying to make a comeback in the final minutes of a championship game, Bobby had some quick decisions to make. He knew he had a chemistry with Ann the likes of no other; and after being so in love and having so much fun the two years they'd dated, he wasn't about to let some other guy knock him out of competition.

That Sunday, April 1st, 1949, Bobby borrowed his father's car and ten dollars from a friend. And as fast as he could run down the football field, he high-tailed it over to Ann's house, instructed her to get ready, and announced they were going for a ride. The Sunday drive that started on 81st Street in East Birmingham ended before a Justice of the Peace in Rising Fawn, Georgia, and the ten dollars Bobby borrowed from his buddy paid for their marriage license.

After the short ceremony, they traveled back home to Birmingham. Because Bobby had to return to the University of Alabama and Ann was still in her senior year at Woodlawn High School, there was no time for a honeymoon. Young and struggling, they could not afford wedding bands so Ann wore Bobby's class ring as a substitute.

For the next four months, Bobby and Ann managed to live apart and keep their marriage a secret. The only people who knew about it were the five other couples that eloped with them. But after four months of silence, word finally leaked out and everybody in Woodlawn heard that Ann and Bobby had been secretly married. Even George Estock, Ann's father, received the information second-hand when Bobby's mother found out and squealed on them.

When Ann's father approached her to confirm the news and she told him it was true, she and Bobby had eloped on April 1st, George Estock hoped his daughter was pulling a belated April Fool's joke on him. Once he discovered she wasn't kidding, he gave Ann no alternative. "Well, if you've got a husband, he needs to take care of you."

At Woodlawn High School, Bobby was the team's key player. But as a freshman at the University of Alabama, he spent most of the football season sitting on the bench and that disappointed him. So instead of Ann moving to Tuscaloosa, Bobby returned to Birmingham and enrolled at Howard College. There he played starting quarterback, was co-captain of the football team, and Little All-American! The situation worked out perfectly because Ann and Bobby lived with his parents rent free until Bobby graduated from college. Upon finishing high school, Ann not only attended Howard College, but made the cheerleading squad there also.

Their impromptu journey to Rising Fawn, Georgia on Sunday, April 1st, 1949 has resulted in over sixty years of marriage, six children, and many grandchildren. The voice that cheered Bobby from the sidelines at Woodlawn High School was the voice that cheered him through college and a successful coaching career. With Ann his biggest supporter, Bobby Bowden led the Florida State Seminoles to triumphant victories from 1976–2009. While he stood on the field and whipped out winning instructions, Ann took charge at home. Day in and day out, she cooked, fed, cleaned, clothed, and refereed their team of children.

Ann Bowden quoted Genesis 2:18: And the Lord God said, "It isn't good for man to be alone; I will make a companion for him, a helper suited to his needs."

She further added: "I really feel my destiny was to be a helpmate to Bobby and help him to achieve what he's achieved in his profession. I believe the Lord chooses people to fulfill just as Christ did in choosing the Disciples, and I think I'm probably what Bobby needed in his personality and make-up. The Lord works in mysterious ways. Sometimes you don't even know when He's working in your life. I look at my life, even from the time I was very, very young; and I know that the Lord had His hand on me even when I didn't know it because I can recall things that were indelibly impressive to me then.

"I remember having an argument with my father at the age of fifteen; I was so angry afterwards, to gain my composure, I walked next door to the Catholic church. The doors were unlocked and I went inside, knelt at the altar and prayed, 'God, please help me to be a good person and make the right decisions in my life. And please help me to live my life according to Your will.'

"When it came time to have a mate, I was only sixteen; but I was ready and never sensed that I wasn't. Bobby's always been my love. Even after I married and throughout our years together, I've never once looked back in regret."

And now a word from her better half: Bobby Bowden believes the love and support he's received from his wife, plus his strong faith in God and love for Him, has attributed to a successful marriage and helped make him a winning coach. "If you can find a truly good wife, she is worth more than precious gems. Her husband can trust her, and she will richly satisfy his needs. She will not hinder him, but help him all her life." (*Proverbs* 31:10-12).

For couples just starting out, and for those who may be in doubt, the former legendary coach of the Florida State Seminoles offers his advice and encouragement:

"Because I've been in the athletic business most all my life, I compare marriage to coaching a football team. You've got to abide by the rules, be willing to make compromises, don't give up, play to win, and stay in the game through thick and thin. Occasionally, somebody is going to get mad and somebody is going to become hurt; but when the going gets tough, never turn your back on the players. If you apply that same advice to your marriage, you and your spouse will come out winners!"

OUT-TAKES

FOR A DIME, SHE'S MINE!
Ann Atkins had many things going for her, but her stunning beauty kept the boys chasing after her. She worked at Birmingham's historical Alabama Theatre, one of the first buildings in Birmingham to have air conditioning installed in the 1930's.

A male friend, Lawyer, worked with her. And his twin brother, Red Sharp, was hired as an engineer. But when Lawyer, asked Ann for a date and Red (who'd had his eye on Ann) found out, Red offered more than a penny for his thoughts. "Lawyer," he bribed. I'll give you a dime and she's mine."

It was during the Great Depression so a dime could buy a gallon of gas among many other things. Thinking it would never go anywhere, Lawyer took the ten cents and Red took his date and later took Ann and as his wife. Their marriage lasted sixty years.

THE POWER OF A MOTHER'S INFLUENCE!

LOLLY LAWSON DIDN'T HAVE ANY attraction to Rufus Ashe, but her mother thought he was an extremely kind and compassionate young man. On several different occasions, Mrs. Lawson would encourage Lolly to ask him out.

YES! In an era (the 1940's) when asking boys out could be viewed as a dating crime, a mom influenced her daughter to ask a male on a date. Finally, to please her mother, Lolly invited Rufus to go on a hayride.

Today, she would advise women to give men they might not think twice about a chance…for she wound up having the time of her life on the hayride. Lolly and Rufus Ashe were married sixty years!

THE BEST MAN

ON THE GRIDIRON, HE COULD perform magic with the football. He was the SEC's sophomore of the year in 1956 and led the SEC with 23 catches for 383 yards as a junior at Auburn. I was proud to be the best friend and roommate of the All-American and NFL all-star Jimmy "Red" Phillips.

But I never could understand how Red managed to play one heck of a football game, yet when it came to dating, he was the most timid and shy man I'd ever known. Being a nice-looking guy with outstanding athletic talent, he had his choice of women, but he'd singled out an Auburn majorette named Mickey Kennedy. The problem was he didn't have the guts to talk to her in a class they had together, much less the nerve to ask her out.

The track team worked out at stadium track and the majorettes had practice at the same place. So one afternoon, Mickey and I were leaving at the same time and I asked if I could walk with her. That's when I had my opportunity to go to bat for my friend. I told her my roommate was "Red" Phillips and he thought she was beautiful but was too shy to strike up a conversation. She said, "Tell him to talk to me."

So I went back to Red and encouraged him to just start by saying hi to Mickey. I could feel for Red. After all, Mickey was extremely striking and could have had dates with any of the four thousand male students at Auburn, but she was delighted that Red had taken an interest in her...almost like she'd secretly had an attraction for him, too.

Red and Mickey went out in his old Chevy, and he was struck in love on their first date. It wasn't too long afterwards, the two of them married. I laugh every time I tell the story. I told it at Jimmy Red's funeral in March 2015 and had everybody chuckling at his celebration of life service.

When you stop and think about it, Jimmy "Red" Phillips had quite a football career. He played seven seasons with the Los Angeles Rams and three with the Minnesota Vikings. He led the NFL with 78 receptions in 1961, the second of his three consecutive Pro Bowl seasons. Red also was named first-team NFL All-Pro that year. During his career, he caught 401 passes for 6,044 yards and 34 touchdowns.

He later coached with the Atlanta Falcons, New Orleans Saints, San Diego Chargers and Florida State Seminoles, yet he was too shy to ask his future bride for a date so I helped him with his passing game on the field of love and stood as his best man at Jimmy Red and Mickey's wedding.

Both have passed on now, but neither of the two will ever be forgotten. Their marriage of fifty-two years and his one heck of a football career is in the history books.

Written by Kathryn Kaufmann as told by Bill Headley

MAYDAY...MAYDAY

LOIS WAS AN ASSISTANT AT a doctor's office and Don was a patient. Fortunately, Don Hassig was healthy and only had to see the doctor once a year. Unfortunately, Lois hoped to see him more. What she didn't know is Don had had his eye on her for a while, but he thought she was married because on one of his visits, she mentioned that her best friend met her husband at the University Club. Don caught the word "husband" and dismissed Lois as a potential assuming she, too, was married.

Not only was the doctor practicing medicine, he was obviously secretly playing matchmaker to the two because six years later during Don's annual check-up, he asked Don about his single status and casually mentioned he had three single nurses working for him. Also, on that visit, he asked Lois to perform a glaucoma test after Don's physical.

Lois found that odd and asked the doctor, "Why? We do not usually do that until a patient is over forty." Don was years from forty. The doctor replied, "He does not know that and it will give you more time in the room with him."

After Don had had a check-up, he called to get the blood test results. When Lois told him how perfect the results were, he suggested they go out to dinner and celebrate. And the years have been dear to Don and Lois Hassig since their wedding on May 1st, 1971.

FROM BLACK DIAMONDS TO WEDDING DIAMONDS

BEING FROM TWO SMALL TOWNS in West Virginia, the chances of two ten year old youngsters from different schools meeting was slim, and yet as I twirled around in my blue and gold Rockets Pop Warner cheerleader skirt, he caught my eye: dressed in black, the quarterback for the opposing team, the Black Diamonds. He didn't seem to notice me and I was tempted to try a cartwheel near him to catch his eye, but I knew my cartwheel was not Grade A caliber, so I tried the old flinging the hair back routine. He definitely didn't notice, and to add insult to injury, his team creamed us.

After the game, busing back to my side of town was like a world away from his side of town, especially at ten years old. Twenty miles and twenty mountains away, I didn't see or hear about Brother Saban (that's what everyone called him, including his family) again until seventh grade YMCA Science Camp where we were each selected by our schools to attend.

Perhaps it was being a member of the Junior Audubon Society or my winning leaf collection that won me the honor of admittance to science camp, but whatever it was, I was happy to be sitting on the bus with Nick on the way to the Dairy Farm. We dissected a frog together and handled snakes and I risked the ultimate by asking him to join me for bird watching at 5:00am the next morning. He was a no show!

Fast forward to high school, where our two football teams were meeting once again; he's still the star quarterback, and I'm still wearing blue and gold but on a majorette uniform. We passed each other on the sideline with a look of acknowledgment and surprise. His team crushed us again, but he was a good sport when he called me that night. Dating our last two years of high school was interrupted when he accepted a football scholarship to Kent State University and I accepted a Teacher›s Scholarship to Fairmont State, but not a day through the week went by that we didn›t write to each other, long letters on notebook paper, saving the phone calls for the weekends when they were less expensive. We were best friends and sweethearts for many years before we married while in college.

And now, 43 years later, we are best friends and sweethearts. It's been a blessing to share my life with Nick, having the same goals and values and enjoying the same things in life. I still bump into him once in a while on the sideline as we enjoy our lives together with our growing family and friends!

~ *Written by Terry Saban*

ABSENCE MAKES THE HEART GROW FONDER

Jane and Joe Kaufmann (featured on the front cover)

NOT AT ALL ENTHUSIASTIC BUT at the insistence of a co-worker, I agreed to meet Joe on a blind date. Finding cigarettes repulsive, I knew the minute he asked if he could smoke and then lit up a Camel after I said "yes," my first date would be my last so I didn't bother to make a big deal out of his smoking habit. But the one thing I got hooked on was Joe's sense of humor and his ability to make me laugh. So when he asked me out for a second date, I accepted.

I wasn't head over heels by any stretch of the imagination, but I enjoyed Joe's company. Then he told me he was soon leaving for Portsmouth, Virginia for the Christmas holidays to visit relatives. Inside, I had a sinking feeling, and it only grew deeper when he stopped calling.

One day shortly after Joe had left town, I went to lunch at Britling's Cafeteria with the girls from work. All of a sudden, while sitting there eating, it hit me that he was gone. I started missing him and realizing I liked him more than I thought. I was thrilled that he finally called me while he was in Virginia. During that conversation, he told me I had a "devil may care attitude." I told him I didn't know I did.

When he returned after his two week visit to Portsmouth, we began to date steady; and after a year and a half, he proposed.

On the evening of my wedding, I began sweating in

the back seat of a neighbor's borrowed air conditioned Cadillac. I suddenly came down with a major case of the nervous jitters and I wanted to bail. My Uncle Marvin opened the back door for me to get out and I expressed, "Take me home. I don't want to get married."

Uncle Marvin shut the door and marched inside the church. I assumed he was going to tell Joe I couldn't follow through with the wedding. But when Uncle Marvin returned to the car, what he told me came as a shock, "Joe isn't here. Nobody has seen him," he exclaimed.

I went into orbit, worrying and waiting to see if he would show and wondering if he didn't, what could have happened. Then I got mad. Mad that he would stand me up at the altar, despite the fact that's exactly what I was about to do to him.

Once I'd pitched my fit about Joe being a no-show, Uncle Marvin confessed, "Joe is in there waiting. But this was a test. I knew if I told you he hadn't yet shown up, you'd make your mind up to marry him if you thought he wasn't available."

Through the smarts of my Uncle Marvin, I made it to the altar and survived thirty-two happy and adventuresome years of marriage to Joe until a massive heart attack took his life on November 20th, 1987.

I've been fortunate to enjoy a happy marriage in my lifetime.

~Written by Kathryn Kaufmann as told by Jane Kaufmann

OTHER BOOK BY KATHRYN

The first of a series, strap on your seatbelt and ride the roller coaster of what life is like as a single. After unexpectedly encountering her old flame, Bradley Gabriel, and placing him on the back burner while trying to decide if she should give their love a second chance, Daisy Fields experiences many dating debacles that lead her to question if she is meant to be with Bradley or meant to be married at all.

Singles will know they are not alone in what can be a cruel world of dating. And married couples just might want to renew their vows after reading about Daisy's experiences in the dating world.

Available Now!

Log on to: *www.datingdaisyfields.com*
and like us on Facebook:
www.facebook.com/kathrynkaufmannwriter?pnref=story

THE
PRIEST
AND THE
Princess
A Novel
When true love brings
sacrifice and suffering.
KJ KAUFMANN

ABOUT THE AUTHOR

I've been told by that I am "eclectic." I don't write just one genre. I can write romance, mystery, humor, self-help, spiritual/inspirational, fiction, nonfiction, articles, and poems. I was even asked to write an obituary and was honored to do so!

Because I am the "go-to girl" and advice guru for my friends, I became a certified life coach. But sometimes…I have to seek help from a coach to get my own life balanced and straightened out. That is normal, right? (I laugh!) But, seriously, due to the lessons I learned in divorce court, having experienced some real doozies in what I call my "dating career," I coached a couple that was on the brink of divorce and they reconciled their marriage. Then I coached a divorced couple, and they began dating again.

I love people! I love life! I love hearing from and communicating with those who reach out to me. I want my writing to touch your life and the lives of those you share me with in a big way. I want you to relate to my work, be moved by my stories, inspired by the power and truth behind the words and become a better person because of it.

To connect with me, view my work or read my blog, please visit me at *www.KatsQuotes.com,* @TheWriteKat via Instagram or Facebook: *www.facebook.com/ kathrynkaufmannwriter?pnref=story*

Love to All,

MARRIAGES MEANT TO BE MEDIA BUZZ:

ABC 33/40, FOX 6 and BIRMINGHAM MAGAZINE

RADIO AND TV INTERVIEWS
WMJJ in Birmingham, Alabama (Magic 96 FM)
FM 100 (Memphis, Tennessee)
98.9 (Tallahassee, Florida)
WHYN (Springfield, Massachusetts)
KVEN (Ventura, California)
WGGY (Scranton, Pennsylvania)
WCXJ (Pittsburgh, Pennsylvania)
WKBN (Youngstown, Ohio)
Late night with Jim Richards (Toronto, Canada)
KVAN, (Vancouver, Washington)
620 AM (Portland, Oregon)
Talk America (Groton, Connecticut)
WELI (New Haven, Connecticut)
WERC (Birmingham, Alabama)
CFPL 98 (London, Ontario, Canada)
Mysteries Around Us (Phoenix, Arizona)
KHBG (Healdsburg, California)
ABC 33/40 Television
Fox 6 Television Morning Show

FEATURE STORY IN
The Birmingham News
The Mobile Register
Article in: The Birmingham Magazine

Made in the USA
Monee, IL
07 July 2026

56549096R00079